Praying the
Promises
Changes Things

Praying the Promises
Changes Things

Lloyd Hildebrand

BRIDGE
LOGOS

Alachua, Florida 32615

Bridge-Logos

Alachua, FL 32615 USA

Praying The Promises Changes Things
by Lloyd Hildebrand

Copyright ©2014 by Lloyd Hildebrand

Printed in the United States of America.

Library of Congress Catalog Card Number:
2014914720

International Standard Book Number:
  978-1-61036-132-3

Unless otherwise noted, all Scripture quotations are
from the King James Version of the Holy Bible.

08-19-14

DEDICATION

TO those throughout the world who are facing persecution, torture, and martyrdom as a result of their faith. Our prayers are with you. We pray that God's words will be your constant source of strength and solace.

CONTENTS

INTRODUCTION

WHEN we learn to pray God's promises from His holy Word, we will see many changes taking place within us and around us. Some of those changes will include:

- A renewed mind
- Growing faith
- Profound joy
- A deeper love for God and others
- Greater confidence in God
- Hope
- Spiritual restoration
- A more-abundant life
- Answered prayer
- Abounding blessings
- And so many more

As a result of these changes, which are miracles wrought by the hand of God, you will witness a multitude of changes taking place among your loved ones, your friends, and your environment.

Yes, *Praying the Promises Changes Things*, and the most important part of this is that it will transform you into a person of commitment, belief, trust, and happiness.

The Bible has much to say about the promises of God—those wonderful commitments that God has made to you. Here are some scriptural passages that reveal His love for us in the form of promises. Remember, His promises never fail.

About God's promises the Bible says:

"For all the promises of God in him are yea, and in him Amen, unto the glory of God by us" (2 Corinthians 1:20).

"Having therefore these promises, dearly beloved, let us cleanse ourselves from all filthiness of the flesh and spirit, perfecting holiness in the fear of God" (2 Corinthians 7:1).

"That ye be not slothful, but followers of them who through faith and patience inherit the promises" (Hebrews 6:12).

"Whereby are given unto us exceeding great and precious promises: that by these ye might be partakers of the divine nature, having escaped the corruption that is in the world through lust" (2 Peter 1:4).

In the above verses we learn a great deal about God's promises. First, God always responds to faith in His promises in the affirmative—a resounding yes! He loves it when His children take their stand upon His promises, which are a key to great blessing in our lives.

As we memorize the promises and learn to walk in them

and upon them, God cleanses us from all filthiness of the flesh, and He enables us to live in holiness before Him and others.

How do we inherit His promises? They are obtained only through faith and patience. We must accept them, believe them, and wait for their fulfillment in our lives.

The promises of God, as we learn to apply them to our lives and receive them into our spirits, enable us to partake of the divine nature, but only after we have renounced all lusts and corruption.

As Adoniram Judson said, "The future is as bright as the promises of God." Based on the promises, therefore, we can say with certainty that our future will be bright. Praise the Lord!

There are more than 3000 promises in God's Word, and it is exceedingly important for you to realize that each of these promises is a personal word from God to you. Everet E. Storms says there are 7,959 promises to claim—almost 8000!

Dwight L. Moody said, "Tarry at a promise and God will meet you there." With this in mind, let us:

- Stand upon God's promises.
- Believe His promises.
- Receive His promises.
- Trust His promises.
- Claim His promises.
- Expect His promises to come true.

Charles Spurgeon, who was known as "the prince of preachers," taught frequently about the promises of God. He said, "It is marvelous, brethren, how one sweet word of God will make whole songs for Christians. One word of God is like a piece of gold, and the Christian is the gold-beater, and he can hammer that promise out for whole weeks. I can say myself, I have lived on one promise for weeks, and want no other. I want just simply to hammer that promise out into gold-leaf, and plate my whole existence with joy from it."

Yes, he has the right idea about the nuggets of gold that the promises of God give to us. As we learn to meditate upon them and pray them, God speaks to us over and over again. He blesses us with His truth, and we are able to receive directly from His heart and His Word.

Part I
Turn Your Back on the Problem and Your Face Toward the Promise

AS you learn to turn your back on the problem and pray the promises, you will discover the power of God's Word to bring transformation to your situation. God already knows what your problems are, so He does not need you to list them. Instead, focus on what He has to say about the problems and the challenges. Speak His promises into existence, as you learn to believe them, receive them, and apply them to your life. Let His Word penetrate your heart and guide you to the answers you seek.

God dispatches His angels to help you get through every situation. He will never let His Word return unto Him void. In order to pray God's Word with faith, we need to trust Him and His promises. We need to accept this truth from the Bible: "All scripture is given by inspiration of God, and is profitable for doctrine, for reproof, for correction, for instruction in righteousness: that the man of God may be perfect, throughly furnished unto all good works" (2 Timothy 3:15-17).

I like that word "throughly," which is hardly ever used. It entails the idea that God's Word works through us and in us through and through. Many people change this to the word "thoroughly," and that certainly applies to God's Word as well. So, when we pray the Scriptures, God's Word washes through us like a stream of water that flows forth into a dark and needy world.

So, turn your back on the problems and focus on God's promise. He will come through for you in His special ways time and time again.

THE PREMISES ON WHICH THE PROMISES ARE BASED

Every promise in God's Word has a premise or a condition upon which it is based. The conditions that are sometimes attached to God's wonderful promises include obedience, faith, trust, and commitment. The important thing to keep in mind is that God promises to bless us when we follow His ways, as they are outlined in His Word.

"Thy word is a lamp unto my feet, and a light unto my path" (Psalm 119:105). Let the light of this bright and beautiful lamp lead you through the darkness of this world. Let it shine upon your pathways and show you how to continue walking with your Lord.

One thing I know for sure: God wants to bless you because He loves you. Take heed to these words from Deuteronomy: "And all these blessings shall come on thee, and overtake thee, if thou shalt hearken unto the voice of the Lord thy God. Blessed shalt thou be in the city, and blessed shalt thou be in the field. Blessed shall be the fruit of thy body, and the fruit of thy ground, and the fruit of thy cattle, the increase of thy kine, and the flocks of thy sheep. . . . Blessed shalt thou be when thou comest in, and blessed shalt thou be when thou goest out. The Lord shall cause thine enemies that rise up against thee to be smitten before thy face: they shall come out against thee one way, and flee before thee seven ways. The Lord shall command the blessing upon thee in thy storehouses, and in all that thou settest thine hand unto; and he shall bless thee in the land which the Lord thy God giveth thee. . . if thou shalt keep the commandments of the Lord thy God, and walk in his ways" (Deuteronomy 28:2–9).

This passage from the Old Testament is filled with God's special promises to you:

- You will experience God's blessings.
- You will be blessed in the town and in the country.
- You will be blessed with productive fields.
- Your flocks and herds will proliferate.
- Your baskets will be overflowing with fruit, and your kneading bowls with bread.

- You will be blessed wherever you go, both coming in and going out.
- The Lord will conquer your enemies.
- You will be blessed in everything you do.
- Your storehouses will be filled with grain.

Though many of these exciting promises are directed to someone who engages in farming, they apply to every one of us. The farming images are metaphors for our own lives; they speak of great abundance and blessing in all aspects of our lives. However, there are some conditions attached to these promises:

- We must obey the Lord.
- We must hearken to the Lord's voice when He speaks to us.
- We must keep His commandments.
- We must walk in His ways.

God's commandments and ways are revealed to us in His holy Word. As we delve into the Bible, we learn what He expects of us. The power of His Spirit is there to help us stand and walk upon His promises in obedience and trust

Why does God want to bless you?

- He wants you to be a blessing to others.
- He wants you to know that He is always there for you.
- He loves you with an everlasting love.

- He wants you to pass His blessings on to your children and grandchildren.
- God wants to have fellowship with you every day.

Our God is a blessing-oriented God. He loves to give good things to His children. Isn't it wonderful to know Him?

Meditate on this promise for a moment: "If ye then, being evil, know how to give good gifts unto your children, how much more shall your Father which is in heaven give good things to them that ask him" (Matthew 7:11). This is a prayer promise that gives us a glimpse into God's good heart.

So, turn your back on the problem and look at God's glorious promises. This will turn you into a triumphant Christian. Let God's miracle-working power flood your being as you pray, and I can assure you that things will change for you. Most importantly, you will change and the promises of God will reveal His will for y ou.

PART II
GOD ALWAYS KEEPS HIS WORD

So shall my word be that goeth forth out of my mouth: it shall not return unto me void, but it shall accomplish that which I please, and it shall prosper in the thing whereto I sent it.
(Isaiah 55:11)

USING GOD'S PROMISES

As I mentioned before, Charles Spurgeon loved the promises of God. I would like you to take a moment to reflect on some of the things he said about the promises:

"God's promises were never meant to be thrown aside as waste paper. He intended them to be used. Nothing pleases our Lord better than to see His promises active in our lives. He loves to see His children bring them up to Him, and say, 'Lord, do as you have promised.'

We glorify God when we plead His promises. Do you think that God will be any the poorer for giving you the riches He promised? Do you dream He will be any the less holy for giving holiness to you? Do you imagine He will be any the less pure for washing you from your sins? He has said, 'Come now, let us reason together. Though your sins are like scarlet, they shall be as white as snow; though they are red as crimson, they shall be like wool.' Faith lays hold upon the promise of pardon, and goes straight to the throne with it, and pleads, 'Lord, here is your promise. Please do as you promised.' To which the Lord replies, 'Your request is granted.' When you get hold of a promise, if you don't take it to God, you dishonor Him. Our heavenly Banker is delighted to cash His own promissory notes. God will not be troubled by your persistently reminding Him of His promises. It is His delight to bestow favors on His children. He is more ready to hear than you are to ask. It is God's nature to keep His promises. Go at once, therefore, to the throne with 'Please do as you promised.'" (From *Morning By Morning,* a Pure Gold Classic published by Bridge–Logos, Inc.)

Please note these facts of faith from the above paragraph:

- God wants you to learn to use His promises.
- Not to take God's promises to Him actually dishonors Him.
- God is not troubled when you remind Him of His promises.
- He delights to bestow favors on His children.

• It is God's nature to keep His promises.

These truths help us to see why praying God's promises is one of the most important things we could ever do.

"NEVER WILL I LEAVE YOU."

In *Morning By Morning* by Charles H. Spurgeon we find this entry for February 23:

"No promise is for private interpretation. Whatever God has said to any one saint, He has said to all. When He opens a well for one, it is so all may drink. When He opens a granary door to give out food [grain], there may be one starving person who is the reason for its being opened, but all hungry saints may come and eat. Whether He gave the word to Abraham or to Moses doesn't matter. He's given it to you also as one of the covenanted seed. There is not a blessing too high for you, or a mercy too great for you. Lift up your eyes to the north and to the south, to the east and to the west, for all this and more is yours. Climb to Pisgah's top, and view the utmost limit of the Promised Land, for the land is all yours. There is not a brook of living water of which you may not drink. If the land flows with milk and honey, eat the honey and drink the milk, for both are yours. But be bold to believe, for He has said, 'Never will I leave you; never will I forsake you.' In this promise God gives to His people everything. 'Never will I leave you.' Then no attribute of God can cease to be active on our behalf. Is He mighty? He

13

will show himself strong on the behalf of those that trust Him. Is He love? Then with loving-kindness He will have mercy upon us—always! 'Never will I leave you; never will I forsake you.'"

Take a moment now to reflect upon these life-giving truths:

- Whatever God has given is for everyone, including you.
- Be bold to believe, for it is faith that inherits the promises. (See Hebrews 6:12.)
- He will never leave you nor forsake you!

MEDITATE UPON GOD'S PROMISES

For the entry of July 27 in *Morning By Morning*, Spurgeon penned these triumphant words about God's faithful promises:

"If you would know experimentally the preciousness of the promises and enjoy them in your own heart, meditate much upon them. Thinking over God's words will often be the prelude to their fulfillment. Many Christians who have thirsted for the fulfillment of a promise have received the blessing they sought even while still meditating on the Word. Besides meditating on the promises, receive them into your soul as the very words of God. Speak to your soul this way: 'If I were dealing with a person's promise, I would carefully consider the ability and the character of the person who made the promise to me. So with the promise of God, I mustn't so much look upon the greatness of the promise, which may stagger me, but upon the greatness of He who promised. That will cheer me. My soul, it's God, even your God, who cannot lie, who speaks to you. This word of His that you are now considering is as true as His own existence. He is an unchangeable God. He has not altered the thing that has gone out of His mouth, nor called back one single comforting sentence. Nor does He lack power, for He who has spoken is the God who made the heavens and the Earth. Nor can He fail in wisdom as to the time when He will give the favors, for He knows when it is best to give and when it's better to withhold. If we meditate upon the promises in this way, and consider the Promiser, we will experience their sweetness and obtain their fulfillment."

What are the key points that Spurgeon stresses in this paragraph?

- To know and enjoy God's promises you must meditate upon them.
- The fulfillment of the promise often comes as we meditate upon the Word.
- We must learn to receive the promises of God.
- God will do what He says, and His power to perform His Word is absolute.
- Meditation enables us to enjoy the sweetness of the promises and to obtain their fulfillment.

GRASP THE PROMISES WITH A PERSONAL, APPROPRIATING FAITH

Charles Spurgeon wrote these words in his devotional classic *Evening By Evening* (entry for October 21):

"'Why sayest thou, O Jacob, and speakest, O Israel, my way is hid from the Lord and my judgment is passed over from my God'? The Lord cares for all things, and the meanest creatures share in His universal providence, but His particular providence is over His saints. 'The angel of the Lord encampeth round about them that fear Him.' 'Precious shall their blood be in His sight.' 'Precious in the sight of the Lord is the death of His saints.' 'We know that all things work together for good to them that love God, to them that are the called according to His purpose.' Let the fact that while He is the Savior of all men, He is specially the Savior of those who believe, cheer, and comfort you. You are His peculiar care, His regal treasure that He guards as the apple of His eye, and His vineyard over which He watches day and night. 'The very hairs of your head are all numbered.' Let the thought of His special love to you be a spiritual painkiller, a dear quietus to your woe: 'I will never leave you, nor forsake you.' God says that as much to you as to any saint of old. 'Fear not, I am your shield, and your exceeding great reward.' We lose much consolation by the habit of reading His promises for the whole church, instead of taking them directly home to ourselves. Believer, grasp the Word with a personal, appropriating faith. Think that you hear Jesus say, 'I have prayed for you that your faith fail not.' Think you see Him walking on the waters of your trouble, for He is there and He is saying, 'Fear not, it is I; be not afraid.' Oh, those sweet words of Christ! May the Holy Ghost make you feel them as spoken to you; forget others for a while—accept the voice of Jesus as addressed to you, and say, 'Jesus whispers consolation; I cannot refuse it; I will sit under His shadow with great delight.'"

These are some of the major points from Spurgeon in the above paragraph:

- You are His regal treasure, and He guards you as the apple of His eye.
- His special love for you is a spiritual painkiller.
- Take His promises as special messages for you and to you.
- Grasp the Word of God with a personal, appropriating faith.

Part III
God Promises to Meet Your Needs

GOD, in the Bible, addresses every human need, and He promises to help us with each one. He always keeps His promises. He cannot fail. I've compiled a list of some of the areas covered by God's promises, along with one promise for each, and, as you will see, the list is quite extensive. Notice how many of the promises have a condition attached to their fulfillment.

Abiding in Christ—"If ye abide in me, and my words abide in you, ye shall ask what ye will, and it shall be done unto you" (John 15:7).

Abundant life—"I am come that they might have life, and that they might have it more abundantly" (John 10:10).

Agreement—"That if two of you shall agree as touching anything that they shall ask, it shall be done for them of my Father which is in heaven" (Matthew 18:19).

Angels—"For he shall give his angels charge over thee, to keep thee in all thy ways. They shall bear thee up in their hands, lest thou dash thy foot against a stone" (Psalm 91:11-12).

Anointing—"But the anointing which ye have received of him abideth in you, and ye need not that any man teach you: but as the same anointing teacheth you of all things, and is truth, and is no lie, and even as it hath taught you, ye shall abide in him" (1 John 2:27).

Answered Prayer—"Thou calledst in trouble, and I delivered thee; I answered thee in the secret place of thunder: I proved thee at the waters of Meribah" (Psalm 81:7).

Atonement—"And not only so, but we also joy in God through our Lord Jesus Christ, by whom we have now received the atonement" (Romans 5:11).

Authority—"For the Son of man is as a man taking a far journey, who left his house, and gave authority to his servants, and to every man his work, and commanded the porter to watch. Watch ye therefore: for ye know not when the master of the house cometh" (Mark 13:34-35).

Beauty—"To appoint unto them that mourn in Zion, to give unto them beauty for ashes, the oil of joy for mourning, the garment of praise for the spirit of heaviness; that they might be called trees of righteousness, the planting of the Lord, that he might be glorified" (Isaiah 61:3).

Believing—"And all things, whatsoever ye shall ask in prayer, believing, ye shall receive" (Matthew 21:22).

Blessing—"The blessing of the Lord, it maketh rich, and he addeth no sorrow with it" (Proverbs 10:22).

Boldness—"According to the eternal purpose which he purposed in Christ Jesus our Lord: in whom we have boldness and access with confidence by the faith of him" (Ephesians 3:11-12).

Broken-heartedness—"The Spirit of the Lord is upon me, because he hath anointed me to preach the gospel to the poor; he hath sent me to heal the brokenhearted, to preach deliverance to the captives, and recovering of sight to the blind, to set at liberty them that are bruised. To preach the acceptable year of the Lord" (Luke 4:18-19).

Burdens—"Cast thy burden upon the Lord, and he shall sustain thee: he shall never suffer the righteous to be moved" (Psalms 55:22).

Calling—"And let the peace of God rule in your hearts, to the which also ye are called in one body; and be ye thankful. Let the word of Christ dwell in you richly in all wisdom" (Colossians 3:15-16).

Caring—"Humble yourselves therefore under the mighty hand of God, that he may exalt you in due time: casting all your care upon him; for he careth for you" (1 Peter 5:6-7).

Change—"But we all, with open face beholding as in a

glass the glory of the Lord, are changed into the same image from glory to glory, even as by the Spirit of the Lord" (2 Corinthians 3:18).

Charity—"And above all these things put on charity, which is the bond of perfectness. And let the peace of God rule in your hearts" (Colossians 3:14-15).

Children—"Train up a child in the way he should go: and when he is old, he will not depart from it" (Proverbs 22:6).

Cleansing—"But if we walk in the light, as he is in the light, we have fellowship one with another, and the blood of Jesus Christ his Son cleanseth us from all sin" (1 John 1:7).

Comfort—"Blessed be the God, even the Father of our Lord Jesus Christ, the Father of mercies, and the God of all comfort; who comforteth us in all our tribulations, that we may be able to comfort them which are in any trouble, by the comfort wherewith we ourselves are comforted of God" (2 Corinthians 1:3-4).

Commandments—"But the mercy of the Lord is from everlasting to everlasting upon them that fear him, and his righteousness unto children's children; to such as keep his covenant, and to those that remember his commandments to do them" (Psalm 103:17-18).

Commitment—"Trust in the Lord, and do good; so shalt thou dwell in the land, and verily thou shalt be fed. Delight thyself also in the Lord; and he shall give thee the desires of thine heart. Commit thy way unto the Lord; trust also in him; and he shall bring it to pass" (Psalm 37:3-5).

Communication—"Let no corrupt communication proceed out of your mouth, but that which is good to the use of edifying, that it may minister grace unto the hearers" (Ephesians 4:29).

Compassion—"But thou, O Lord, art a God full of compassion, and gracious, longsuffering, and plenteous in mercy and truth. O turn unto me, and have mercy upon me; give thy strength unto thy servant" (Psalm 86:15-16).

Confession—"Confess your faults one to another, and pray one for another, that ye may be healed. The effectual fervent prayer of a righteous man availeth much" (James 5:16).

Confidence—"For thus saith the Lord God, the Holy One of Israel; in returning and rest shall ye be saved; in quietness and in confidence shall be your strength" (Isaiah 30:15).

Consolation—"Now our Lord Jesus Christ himself, and God, even our Father, which hath loved us, and hath given us everlasting consolation and good hope through grace, comfort your hearts and stablish you in every good word and work" (2 Thessalonians 2:16-17).

Contentment—"But godliness with contentment is great gain" (1 Timothy 6:6).

Conversion—"Restore unto me the joy of thy salvation;

and uphold me with thy free spirit. Then will I teach transgressors thy ways; and sinners shall be converted unto thee" (Psalm 51:12-13).

Correction—"All scripture is given by inspiration of God, and is profitable for doctrine, for reproof, for correction, for instruction in righteousness: that the man of God may be perfect, throughly furnished unto all good works" (2 Timothy 3:16-17).

Covenant—"Now the God of peace, that brought again from the dead our Lord Jesus, that great shepherd of the sheep, through the blood of the everlasting covenant, make you perfect in every good work to do his will, working in you that which is well pleasing in his sight, through Jesus Christ; to whom be glory for ever and ever. Amen" (Hebrews 13:20-21).

Death—"But is now made manifest by the appearing of our Saviour Jesus Christ, who hath abolished death, and hath brought life and immortality to light through the gospel" (2 Timothy 1:10).

Delight—"But his delight is in the law of the Lord; and in his law doth he meditate day and night. And he shall be like a tree planted by the rivers of water, that bringeth forth his fruit in his season; his leaf also shall not wither; and whatsoever he doeth shall prosper" (Psalm 1:2-3).

Deliverance—"He hath delivered my soul in peace from the battle that was against me" (Psalm 55:18).

Desires—"Delight thyself also in the Lord; and he shall

24

give thee the desires of thine heart" (Psalm 37:4).

Diligence—"The hand of the diligent maketh rich" (Proverbs 10:4).

Discipleship—"Herein is my Father glorified, that ye bear much fruit; so shall ye be my disciples. As the Father hath loved me, so have I loved you: continue ye in my love. If ye keep my commandments, ye shall abide in my love; even as I have kept my father's commandments, and abide in his love" (John 15:8-10).

Disease—"If thou wilt diligently hearken to the voice of the Lord thy God, and wilt do that which is right in his sight, and wilt give ear to his commandments, and keep all his statutes, I will put none of these diseases upon thee, which I have brought upon the Egyptians: for I am the Lord that healeth thee" (Exodus 15:26).

Distress—"For thou hast been a strength to the poor, a strength to the needy in his distress, a refuge from the storm, a shadow from the heat, when the blast of the terrible ones is as a storm against the wall" (Isaiah 25:5).

Edification—"But speaking the truth in love, may grow up into him in all things, which is the head, even Christ: from whom the whole body fitly joined together and compacted by that which every joint supplieth, according to the effectual working in the measure of every part, making increase of the body unto the edifying of itself in love" (Ephesians 4:15-16).

Endurance—"But he that shall endure unto the end, the same shall be saved" (Matthew 24:13).

Enemies—"For in the time of trouble he shall hide me in his pavilion: in the secret of his tabernacle shall he hide me; he shall set me upon a rock. And now shall mine head be lifted up above mine enemies round about me: therefore will I offer in his tabernacle sacrifices of joy; I will sing, yea, I will sing praises unto the Lord" (Psalm 27:5–6).

Everlasting life—"For God so loved the world, that he gave his only begotten Son, that whosoever believeth in him should not perish, but have everlasting life" (John 3:16).

Expectation—"According to my earnest expectation and my hope, that in nothing I shall be ashamed, but that with all boldness, as always, so now also Christ shall be magnified in my body, whether it be by life, or by death. For to me to live is Christ, and to die is gain" (Philippians 2:20–21).

Faith—"That the trial of your faith, being much more precious than of gold that perisheth, though it be tried with fire, might be found unto praise and honour and glory at the appearing of Jesus Christ: whom having not seen, ye love; in whom, though now ye see him not, yet believing, ye rejoice with joy unspeakable and full of glory: receiving the end of your faith, even the salvation of your souls" (1 Peter 1:7–9).

Faithfulness—"O love the Lord, all ye his saints: for the Lord preserveth the faithful, and plentifully rewardeth the proud doer. Be of good courage, and he shall strengthen your heart, all ye that hope in the Lord" (Psalm 33:23–24).

Fasting—"And when he was come into the house, his disciples asked him privately, why could we not cast him out? And he said unto them, This kind can come forth by nothing, but by prayer and fasting" (Mark 9:28–29).

Favor—"For thou, Lord, wilt bless the righteous; with favour wilt thou compass him as with a shield" (Psalm 5:12).

Fear—"There is no fear in love; but perfect love casteth out fear: because fear hath torment. He that feareth is not made perfect in love" (1 John 4:18).

Fellowship—"That which we have seen and heard declare we unto you, that ye also may have fellowship with us: and truly our fellowship is with the Father, and with his Son Jesus Christ. And these things write we unto you, that your joy may be full. . . .But if we walk in the light as he is in the light, we have fellowship one with another, and the blood of Jesus Christ cleanseth us from all sin" (1 John 1:3–7).

Forgiveness—"If we confess our sins, he is faithful and just to forgive us our sins, and to cleanse us from all unrighteousness" (1 John 1:9).

Freedom—"If the Son therefore shall make you free, ye shall be free indeed." (John 8:36).

Gentleness—"But the fruit of the Spirit is love, joy, peace, longsuffering, gentleness, goodness, faith, meekness, temperance: against such there is no law. And they that are Christ's have crucified the flesh with the affections and lusts" (Galatians 5:22–24).

Giving—"Every man according as he purposeth in his heart, so let him give; not grudgingly, or of necessity: for God loveth a cheerful giver" (2 Corinthians 9:7).

Gladness—"Thou hast loved righteousness and hated iniquity; therefore God, even thy God, hath anointed thee with the oil of gladness above thy fellows" (Hebrews 1:9).

Glory—"According as his divine power hath given unto us all things that pertain unto life and godliness, through the knowledge of him that hath called us to glory and virtue; whereby are given unto us exceeding great and precious promises: that by these ye might be partakers of the divine nature, having escaped the corruption that is in the world through lust" (2 Peter 1:4).

Godliness—"But godliness with contentment is great gain" (1 Timothy 6:6).

Goodness—"For the fruit of the Spirit is in all goodness and righteousness and truth; proving what is acceptable unto the Lord" (Ephesians 5:9-10).

Growth—"The righteous shall flourish like the palm tree: he shall grow like a cedar in Lebanon" (Psalm 92:12).

Guidance—"I will instruct thee and teach thee in the way which thou shalt go: I will guide thee with mine eye" (Psalm 32:8).

Healing—"But unto you, that fear my name shall the Sun of righteousness arise with healing in his wings;

and ye shall go forth, and grow up as calves of the stall" (Malachi 4:2).

Health—"For I will restore health unto thee, and I will heal thee of thy wounds, saith the Lord" (Jeremiah 30:17).

Heaven—"Blessed be the God and Father of our Lord Jesus Christ, which according to his abundant mercy hath begotten us again unto a lively hope by the resurrection of Jesus Christ from the dead, to an inheritance incorruptible, and undefiled, and that fadeth not away, reserved in heaven for you, who are kept by the power of God through faith unto salvation ready to be revealed in the last time" (1 Peter 1:3-4).

Heaviness—"To appoint unto them that mourn in Zion, to give unto them beauty for ashes, the oil of joy for mourning, the garment of praise for the spirit of heaviness; that they might be called trees of righteousness, the planting of the Lord, that he might be glorified" (Isaiah 61:3).

Holiness—"The oath which he sware to our father Abraham, that he would grant unto us, that we being delivered out of the hand of our enemies might serve him without fear, in holiness and righteousness before him, all the days of our life" (Luke 1:73-75).

Holy Spirit—"And hope maketh not ashamed; because the love of God is shed abroad in our hearts by the Holy Ghost which is given unto us" (Romans 5:5).

Honor—"By humility and the fear of the Lord are riches, and honour, and life" (Proverbs 22:4).

Hope—"Looking for that blessed hope, and the glorious appearing of the great God and our Saviour Jesus Christ; who gave himself for us, that he might redeem us from all iniquity, and purify unto himself a peculiar people, zealous of good works" (Titus 2:13-14).

Humility—"By humility and the fear of the Lord are riches, and honour, and life" (Proverbs 22:4).

Imaginations—"For the weapons of our warfare are not carnal, but mighty through God to the pulling down of strongholds; casting down imaginations, and every high thing that exalteth itself against the knowledge of God, and bringing into captivity every thought to the obedience of Christ" (2 Corinthians 10:5).

Immortality—"For this corruptible must put on incorruption, and this mortal must put on immortality. So when this corruptible shall have put on incorruption, and this mortal shall have put on immortality, then shall be brought to pass the saying that is written, Death is swallowed up in victory. O death, where is thy sting? O grave, where is thy victory? The sting of death is sin; and the strength of sin is the law. But thanks be to God, which giveth us the victory through our Lord Jesus Christ" (1 Corinthians 15:53-57).

Inheritance—"In whom also we have obtained an inheritance, being predestinated according to the purpose of him who worketh all things after the counsel of his own will: that we should be to the praise of his glory, who first trusted in Christ" (Ephesians 1:11-12).

Joy—"The joy of the Lord is your strength" (Nehemiah 8:10).

Justification—"But for us also, to whom it shall be imputed, if we believe on him that raised up Jesus our Lord from the dead; who was delivered for our offences, and was raised for our justification" (Romans 4:24-25).

Kindness—"For the mountains shall depart, and the hills be removed; but my kindness shall not depart from thee, neither shall the covenant of my peace be removed, saith the Lord that hath mercy on thee" (Isaiah 54:10).

Knowledge—"Yea, if thou criest after knowledge, and liftest up thy voice for understanding; if thou sleekest her as silver, and searchest for her as for hid treasures: then shalt thou understand the fear of the Lord, and find the knowledge of God" (Proverbs 2:3-5).

Leading—"Hear my cry, O God; attend unto my prayer. From the end of the earth will I cry unto thee, when my heart is overwhelmed: lead me to the rock that is higher than I. For thou hast been a shelter for me, and a strong tower from the enemy" (Psalm 61:1-3).

Life—"Verily, verily, I say unto you, he that believeth on me hath everlasting life. I am the bread of life" (John 6:47-48).

Love—"He will love thee, and bless thee, and multiply thee: he will also bless the fruit of thy womb, and the fruit of thy land, thy corn, and thy wine, and thine oil, the increase of thy kine, and the flocks of thy sheep in the land which he sware unto thy fathers to give thee. Thou shalt be blessed above all people" (Deuteronomy 7:13-14).

Loving-kindness—"The Lord hath appeared of old unto me, saying, Yea, I have loved thee with an everlasting love: therefore with lovingkindness have I drawn thee" (Jeremiah 31:3).

Marriage—"Therefore shall a man leave his father and his mother, and shall cleave unto his wife: and they shall be one flesh" (Genesis 2:24).

Meditation—"Blessed is the man that walketh not in the counsel of the ungodly, nor standeth in the way of sinners, nor sitteth in the seat of the scornful. But his delight is in the law of the Lord; and in his law doth he meditate day and night. And he shall be like a tree planted by the rivers of water, that bringeth forth his fruit in his season; his leaf also shall not wither; and whatsoever he doeth shall prosper" (Psalm 1:1-3).

Meekness—"Blessed are the meek: for they shall inherit the earth" (Matthew 5:5).

Mercy—"For thou, Lord, art good, and ready to forgive; and plenteous in mercy unto all them that call upon thee" (Psalm 86:5).

Might—"Not by might, nor by power, but by my spirit, saith the Lord of hosts" (Zechariah 4:6).

Ministry—"And all things are of God, who hath reconciled us to himself by Jesus Christ, and hath given to us the ministry of reconciliation; to wit, that God was in Christ, reconciling the world unto himself, not imputing their trespasses unto them; and hath committed unto us the word of reconciliation. Now then we are ambassadors for Christ, as though God did beseech you by us: we pray you in Christ's stead, be ye reconciled to God. For he hath made him to be sin for us who knew no sin: that we might be made the righteousness of God in him" (2 Corinthians 5:18–21).

Mourning—"Thou hast turned for me my mourning into dancing: thou hast put off my sackcloth, and girded me with gladness; to the end that my glory may sing praise to thee, and not be silent. O Lord my God, I will give thanks unto thee for ever" (Psalm 30:11–12).

Mysteries—"Unto you it is given to know the mysteries of the kingdom of God: but to others in parables; that seeing they might not see, and hearing they might not understand" (Luke 8:10).

Needs—"But my God shall supply all your need according to his riches in glory by Christ Jesus" (Philippians 4:19).

Obtaining—"In whom we have obtained an inheritance, being predestinated according to the purpose of him who worketh all things after the counsel of his own will" (Ephesians 1:11).

Offerings—"Will a man rob God? Yet ye have robbed me. But ye say, Wherein have we robbed thee? In tithes and offerings. . . . Bring ye all the tithes into the storehouse, that there may be meat in mine house, and prove me now herewith, saith the Lord of hosts, if I will not open you the windows of heaven, and pour you out a blessing, that there shall not be room enough to receive it" (Malachi 3:8-10).

Old Age—"Who satisfieth thy mouth with good things; so that thy youth is renewed like the eagle's" (Psalm 103:4).

Pardon—"The good Lord pardon every one that prepareth his heart to seek God" (2 Chronicles 30:18-19).

Pastors—"And I will give you pastors according to mine heart, which shall feed you with knowledge and understanding" (Jeremiah 3:15).

Peace—"For he is our peace, who hath made both one, and hath broken down the middle wall of partition between us" (Ephesians 2:14).

Perfection—"Out of Zion, the perfection of beauty, God hath shined. Our God shall come, and shall not keep silence: a fire shall devour before him, and it shall be very tempestuous round about him" (Psalm 50:2-3).

Persecution—"Who shall separate us from the love of Christ? Shall tribulation, or distress, or persecution, or famine, or nakedness, or peril, or sword? . . . .Nay, in all these things we are more than conquerors through him that loved us" (Romans 8:35-37).

Pleasures—"Thou wilt shew me the path of life: in thy presence is fullness of joy; at thy right hand there are pleasures for evermore" (Psalm 16:11).

Praise—"But thou art holy, O thou that inhabitest the praises of Israel" (Psalm 22:3).

Prayer—"For every creature of God is good, and nothing to be refused, if it be received with thanksgiving: for it is sanctified by the word of God and prayer" (1 Timothy 4:4-5).

Preaching—"It pleased God by the foolishness of preaching to save them that believe" (1 Corinthians 1:21).

Presence—"My presence shall go with thee, and I will give thee rest" (Exodus 33:14).

Promises—"For all the promises of God in him are yea, and in him Amen, unto the glory of God by us" (2 Corinthians 1:20).

Prophecy—"We have a more sure word of prophecy: whereunto ye do well that ye take heed, as unto a light that shineth in a dark place, until the day dawn, and the day star arise in your hearts" (2 Peter 1:19).

Prosperity—"Let them shout for joy, and be glad, that favour my righteous cause: yea, let them say continually, let the Lord be magnified, which hath pleasure in the prosperity of his servant" (Psalm 35:27).

Provision—"This is my rest for ever: here will I dwell; for I have desired it. I will abundantly bless her provision: I will satisfy her poor with bread" (Psalm 132:15).

Prudence—"In whom we have redemption through his

blood, the forgiveness of sins, according to the riches of his grace; wherein he hath abounded toward us in all wisdom and prudence; having made known unto us the mystery of his will, according to his good pleasure which he hath purposed in himself" (Ephesians 1:7-9).

Purity—"With the merciful thou wilt shew thyself merciful; with an upright man thou wilt shew thyself upright; with the pure thou wilt shew thyself pure. . . .for thou wilt light my candle; the Lord my God will enlighten my darkness" (Psalm 18:25-28).

Purpose—"And we know that all things work together for good to them that love God, to them who are the called according to his purpose" (Romans 8:28).

Quickening—"For Christ also hath once suffered for sins, the just for the unjust, that he might bring us to God, being put to death in the flesh, but quickened by the Spirit" (1 Peter 3:18).

Quietness—"For thus saith the Lord God, the Holy One of Israel; in returning and rest shall ye be saved; in quietness and in confidence shall be your strength" (Isaiah 30:15).

Reaping—"They that sow in tears shall reap in joy" (Psalm 126:5).

Receiving—"With good will doing service, as to the Lord, and not to men: knowing that whatsoever good thing any man doeth, the same shall he receive of the Lord, whether he be bond or free" (Ephesians 6:7-8).

Redemption—"Being justified freely by his grace through the redemption that is in Christ Jesus" (Romans 3:24).

Reigning—"For if by one man's offence death reigned by one; much more they which receive abundance of grace and of the gift of righteousness shall reign in life by one, Jesus Christ" (Romans 5:17).

Rejoicing—"He that goeth forth and weepeth, bearing precious seed, shall doubtless come again with rejoicing, bringing his sheaves with him" (Psalm 126:6).

Restoration—"For I will restore health unto thee, and I will heal thee of thy wounds" (Jeremiah 30:17).

Resurrection—"Blessed be the God and Father of our Lord Jesus Christ, which according to his abundant mercy hath begotten us again unto a lively hope by the resurrection of Jesus Christ from the dead, to an inheritance incorruptible, and undefiled, and that fadeth not away, reserved in heaven for you, who are kept by the power of God through faith unto salvation ready to be revealed in the last time" (1 Peter 1:3-5).

Reverence—"Wherefore we are receiving a kingdom which cannot be moved, let us have grace, whereby we may serve God acceptably with reverence and godly fear: for our God is a consuming fire" (Hebrews 12:28-29).

Righteousness—"And if Christ be in you, the body is dead because of sin; but the Spirit is life because of righteousness" (Romans 8:10).

Sacrifices—"The sacrifices of God are a broken spirit: a broken and a contrite heart, O God, thou wilt not despise" (Psalm 51:17).

Saints—"And he that searcheth the hearts knoweth what is the mind of the Spirit, because he maketh intercession for the saints according to the will of God" (Romans 8:27).

Salvation—"The Lord liveth; and blessed be my rock; and exalted be the God of the rock of my salvation" (2 Samuel 22:47).

Sanctification—"And the very God of peace sanctify you wholly; and I pray God y our whole spirit and soul and body be preserved blameless unto the coming of our Lord Jesus Christ. Faithful is he that calleth you, who also will do it" (1 Thessalonians 5:23-24).

Satisfaction—"He shall call upon me, and I will answer him: I will be with him in trouble; I will deliver him, and honour him. With long life will I satisfy him, and shew him my salvation" (Psalm 91:15-16).

Searching—"Yea, if thou criest after knowledge, and liftest up thy voice for understanding; if thou sleekest her as silver, and searchest for her as for hid treasures: then shalt thou understand the fear of the Lord, and find the knowledge of God" (Proverbs 2:3-5).

Seeking—"But seek ye first the kingdom of God, and his righteousness; and all these things shall be added unto you. Take therefore no thought for the morrow; for the morrow shall take thought for the things of itself. Sufficient unto the day is the evil thereof" (Matthew 6:33-34).

Serving—"I beseech you therefore , brethren, by the mercies of God, that ye present your bodies a living sacrifice, holy, acceptable unto God, which is your reasonable service. And be not conformed to this world: but be ye transformed by the renewing of your mind, that ye may prove what is that good, and acceptable and perfect, will of God" (Romans 12:1-2).

Signs—"And these signs shall follow them that believe; in my name shall they cast out devils; they shall speak with new tongues; they shall take up serpents; and if they drink any deadly thing, it shall not hurt them: they shall lay hands on the sick, and they shall recover" (Mark 16:17-18).

Simplicity—"Gracious is the Lord, and righteous; yea, our God is merciful. The Lord preserveth the simple I was brought low, and he helped me. Return unto thy rest, O my soul; for the Lord hath dealt bountifully with thee" (Psalm 116:5-7).

Sincerity—"And this I pray, that your love may abound yet more and more in knowledge and in all judgment; that ye may approve things that are excellent; that ye may be sincere and without offence till the day of Christ; being filled with the fruits of righteousness, which are by Jesus Christ, unto the glory and praise of God" (Philippians 1:9-11).

Singing—"The Lord thy God in the midst of thee is

mighty; he will save, he will rejoice over thee with joy; he will rest in his love, he will joy over thee with singing" (Zephaniah 3:17).

Spirituality—"For to be carnally minded is death; and to be spiritually minded is life and peace" (Romans 8:6).

Strength—"'My grace is sufficient for thee: for my strength is made perfect in weakness.' Most gladly therefore will I rather glory in my infirmities, that the power of Christ may rest upon me" (2 Corinthians 12:9).

Suffering—"For I reckon that the sufferings of this present time are not worthy to be compared with the glory which shall be revealed in us" (Romans 8:18).

Teaching—"Shew me thy ways, O Lord; teach me thy paths. Lead me in thy truth, and teach me: for thou art the God of my salvation; on thee do I wait all the day" (Psalm 25:4–5).

Temptation—"There hath no temptation taken you but such as is common to man: but God is faithful, who will not suffer you to be tempted above that ye are able; but will with the temptation also make a way to escape, that ye may be able to bear it" (1 Corinthians 10:13).

Thanksgiving—"And let the peace of God rule in your hearts, to the which also ye are called in one body; and be ye thankful. Let the word of Christ dwell in you richly in all wisdom; teaching and admonishing one another in psalms and hymns and spiritual songs, singing with grace in your hearts to the Lord. And whatsoever ye do in word or deed, do all in the name of the Lord

Jesus, giving thanks to God and the Father by him" (Colossians 3:15-17).

Thirst—"But whosoever drinketh of the water that I shall give him shall never thirst; but the water that I shall give him shall be in him a well of water springing up into everlasting life" (John 4:14).

Thoughts—"For the word of God is quick, and powerful, and sharper than any twoedged sword, piercing even to the dividing asunder of soul and spirit, and of the joints and marrow, and is a discerner of the thoughts and intents of the heart" (Hebrews 4:12).

Tongue—"My tongue shall speak of thy word: for all thy commandments are righteousness" (Psalm 119:172).

Treasures—"That their hearts might be comforted, being knit together in love, and unto all riches of the full assurance of understanding, to the acknowledgement of the Father, and of Christ; in whom are hid all the treasures of wisdom and knowledge" (Colossians 2:2-3).

Trials—"That the trial of your faith, being much more precious than of gold that perisheth, though it be tried with fire, might be found unto praise and honour and glory at the appearing of Jesus Christ: whom having not seen, ye love; in whom, though now ye see him not, yet believing, ye rejoice with joy unspeakable and full of glory: receiving the end of your faith, even the salvation of your souls" (1 Peter 1:7-9).

Triumph—"Now thanks be unto God, which always causeth us to triumph in Christ, and maketh manifest the savour of his knowledge by us in every place" (2 Corinthians 2:14).

Trust—"Trust in the Lord with all thine heart; and lean not unto thine own understanding. In all thy ways acknowledge him, and he shall direct thy paths" (Proverbs 3:5-6).

Understanding—"That the God of our Lord Jesus Christ, the Father of glory, may give unto you the spirit of wisdom and revelation in the knowledge of him: the eyes of your understanding being enlightened; that ye may know what is the hope of his calling, and what the riches of the glory of his inheritance in the saints" (Ephesians 1:18).

Uprightness—"O keep my soul, and deliver me: let me not be ashamed; for I put my trust in thee. Let integrity and uprightness preserve me; for I wait on thee" (Psalm 25:20-21).

Victory—"For whatsoever is born of God overcometh the world: and this is the victory that overcometh the world, even our faith" (1 John 5:4).

Vision—"Where there is no vision, the people perish: but he that keepeth the law, happy is he" (Proverbs 29:18).

Waiting—"And not only they, but ourselves also, which have the firstfruits of the Spirit, even we ourselves groan within ourselves, waiting for the adoption, to wit, the redemption of our body" (Romans 8:23).

Weakness—"My grace is sufficient for thee: for my

strength is made perfect in weakness" (2 Corinthians 12:9).

Weariness—"And let us not grow weary in well doing: for in due season we shall reap, if we faint not" (Galatians 6:9).

Wisdom—"Happy is the man that findeth wisdom, and the man that getteth understanding" (Proverbs 3:13).

Witnessing—"But ye shall receive power, after that the Holy Ghost is come upon you: and ye shall be witnesses unto me" (Acts 1:8).

Wonders—"And it shall come to pass afterward, that I will pour out my spirit upon all flesh; and your sons and your daughters shall prophesy, your old men shall dream dreams, your young men shall see visions: and also upon the servants and upon the handmaids in those days will I pour out my spirit. And I will shew wonders in the heavens and in the earth, blood, and fire, and pillars of smoke" (Joel 2:28–30).

Work—"Therefore, my beloved brethren, be ye stedfast, unmoveable, always abounding in the work of the Lord, forasmuch as ye know that your labour is not in vain in the Lord" (1 Corinthians 15:58).

Worship—"God is a Spirit; and they that worship him must worship him in spirit and in truth" (John 4:24).

Youth—"Remember now thy Creator in the days of thy youth, while the evil days come not, nor the years draw nigh, when thou shalt say, I have no pleasure in them" (Ecclesiastes 12:1).

Zeal—"Looking for that blessed hope, and the glorious appearing of the great God and our Saviour Jesus Christ; who gave himself for us, that he might redeem us from all iniquity, and purify unto himself a peculiar people, zealous of good works" (Titus 2:14-15).

Part IV
Praying the Promises

THE prayers in this section of the book are based on God's promises as they are recorded in His Word. As you pray them, your faith will grow, and you will be able to reach out and appropriate God's promises to meet your particular needs.

The prayers are arranged alphabetically and topically for easy reference. I hope you will pray them over and over again and let God's Word fill you, change you, direct you, and keep you. May you be greatly blessed as you read, meditate, and pray.

1
ABIDING IN THE LORD

*If ye abide in me, and my words abide in you,
ye shall ask what ye will, and it
shall be done unto you.*
(John 15:7)

Central Focus: Abiding entails remaining, enduring, waiting, submitting to, and continuing without change. As we learn to abide in Christ and let His words abide in us, amazingly wonderful things will always happen.

A Promise From God: "If ye keep my commandments, ye shall abide in my love, even as I have kept my Father's commandments and abide in his love" (John 15:10).

Prayer: O Lord, my God, show me how to abide constantly in Christ and to let His words abide in me, for I know that, as I learn to stay there, you will answer my prayers and you will bless me. Thank you, Father. With your help, I will learn to abide in Christ, for I know that this is the key to great fruitfulness in my life. I realize, Father, that without Him I can do nothing, but through Him I can do all things. Hallelujah!

As I learn to abide in Christ, I ask that you would help me to walk as He walked. I want your Word to abide in me, Father, for I know this will enable me to overcome the wicked one at all times. I want your anointing to abide in me and to teach me of all things. Thank you so much for the privilege I have of being able to abide in Christ.

Through your grace, Father, I will dwell in the secret place and I will abide under your shadow. Thank you for this precious promise from your Word and for all your promises. I will let them abide in me.

Thank you for the Holy Spirit, who is my Comforter; I know He will abide with me forever. Father, I desire to abide in your love at all times even as Jesus kept your commandments and abided in your love. Help me to ever be your obedient servant.

Thank you for calling me, Father; may I ever abide in your calling. It is my heart's desire to abide with you forever.

Abiding in you and with you brings great joy to my heart. I will ever abide in your love, Father.

In Jesus' name I pray, Amen.

Scriptures: John 15:7; John 15:5; Philippians 4:13; 1 John 2:6; 1 John 2:14; 1 John 2:27; Psalm 91:1; John 14:16; John 15:10; 1 Corinthians 7:20; 1 Corinthians 7:24.

Personal Affirmation: I will constantly abide in Christ. I will memorize His Word so that His words will always abide in me. Both these forms of abiding assure me that God will take care of me and bless me in all that I do.

Meditation: *"God is most glorified in us when we are most satisfied in Him"* (John Piper).

———— ✣ ————

2
ABUNDANCE

I am come that they might have life, and that they might have it more abundantly. (John 10:10)

Central Focus: Abundantly living is ours in the here-and-now. Jesus came to help us find His abundance in this life. He gives from His abundance so that we could live abundantly in Him throughout our lives.

A Promise From God: "Blessed be the God and Father of our Lord Jesus Christ, which according to his abundant mercy hath begotten us again unto a lively hope by the resurrection of Jesus Christ from the dead" (1 Peter 1:3).

Prayer: Thank you, Father, for sending Jesus to give me abundant life. I will walk in abundant life from this point forward. How excellent is your loving-kindness, O God! I put my unwavering trust in you as I live in the shadow of your wings. Thank you for abundantly satisfying me with treasures from your house. I am so thankful that you have enabled me to drink from the river of your pleasures.

Thank you for your promise to always do exceeding abundantly above all that I could ever ask or think, according to your power which is at work within me. As I trust in you, O Lord, and endeavor to do good, I know you will take care of me. I commit my way to you, and I thank you for the abundance you've given to me. I take great delight in the abundance of peace you've given to me.

Thank you, Lord, for giving me the knowledge of your mysteries. This is true spiritual abundance. Thank you for your promise that states that you will give more abundance to me. I receive it now in Jesus' name. As I seek first your kingdom and your righteousness, I know that you will add all other things unto me. Thank you, Father.

It thrills me to know that you will supply all my needs according to your riches in glory by Christ Jesus. Hallelujah! Thank you for the abundance of your grace and the gift of righteousness which have come to me through Jesus Christ. I know I shall ever reign with Him.

Thank you for giving me abundant joy. You are the Lord God, and you are merciful, gracious, longsuffering, and abundant in goodness and grace. I receive from your abundance as I pray, and I will ever be thankful unto you.

I seek you while you may be found, and I seek your marvelous abundance in my life, Lord God. I forsake all selfish ways and thoughts, as I return to you, Lord, and I know you are having mercy on me and you are abundantly pardoning me.

Thank you so much for your kindness and love. It is not by works of righteousness that I've done, but it is according to your mercy that I have been saved. Thank you, Father, for the washing of regeneration and renewing of the Holy Ghost, which you've abundantly shed on me through Jesus Christ, my Savior.

My heart is filled with gratitude for the abundance you've given to me, Father.

In Jesus' name, Amen.

Scriptures: John 10:10; Psalm 36:7-8; Psalm 37:3-5; Psalm 35:11; Matthew 13:11-12; Matthew 6:33; Philippians 4:19; Romans 5:17; 2 Corinthians 8:2; Exodus 34:6; Isaiah 55:6-7; Titus 3:4-6.

Personal Affirmation: Abundant living is mine to enjoy in the here-and-now. May I never do anything that would block that abundance from my life. I have received so much from God's abundance. His abundant life supplies all that I need.

Meditation: *"Always, everywhere God is present, and always He seeks to discover himself to each one"* (A.W. Tozer).

3

AFFLICTIONS

Is any among you afflicted? Let him pray. Is any merry? Let him sing psalms. (James 5:13)

Central Focus: God is with me during every affliction, trial, and difficulty. His strength is made perfect in my weakness.

A Promise From God: "For our light affliction, which is but for a moment, worketh for us a far more exceeding and eternal weight of glory" (2 Corinthians 4:17).

Prayer: O Lord, my God, during this time of affliction I reach out to you. Turn unto me and have mercy upon me, for I am desolate and afflicted. The troubles of my heart are enlarged. O bring me out of my distresses. Look upon my affliction and my pain, and forgive me of all my sins.

Thank you for regarding my affliction, Father, and hearing my cry. I thank you for your Word and all its promises which are my comfort during this affliction. O Lord, you are my strength and my fortress. Thank you for being my refuge during affliction.

I will not faint, Father, during this affliction. Even though my outer man perishes, I know you are renewing my inner man day by day. Thank you, Lord. This light affliction that I am going through is but for a moment, and I know it is working for me a far more

PRAYING THE PROMISES CHANGES THINGS

exceeding and eternal weight of glory. I will not look at the things which are seen, but at the things which are not seen, because I know that the things that are seen are temporary, but the things that are unseen are eternal. Thank you, Father, for this wonderful promise from your Word.

Thank you for the Gospel of Jesus Christ, which has come to me in both word and power and in the Holy Ghost and assurance. I will be your follower, Lord, even during this time of affliction, because I know your Word and I have joy in the Holy Ghost. Hallelujah!

Like Moses, I would rather suffer affliction than to enjoy the pleasures of sin even for a season. Thank you for the example of the prophets who spoke in your name and showed how to suffer affliction with patience and endurance. I'm sure they were happy in you as they endured affliction, and I would like to be like them.

Your Word tells me that many are the afflictions of the righteous, but you deliver us out of them all. I thank you, Lord, that you are delivering me out of this present affliction. I praise your name. I reckon through faith that the sufferings of this present time are not worthy to be compared to the glory that I know you will reveal. Thank you, Lord.

Thank you for imparting your righteousness to me through Christ. I desire to know you and the power of your resurrection and the fellowship of your sufferings, and to be made conformable to the death of Christ.

I choose to rejoice, Lord, inasmuch as I am a partaker of Christ's sufferings. I know that when His glory shall be revealed, I will be glad with exceeding joy.

In the blessed name of Jesus I pray, Amen.

Scriptures: Psalm 25:16-18; Psalm 106:44; Psalm 119:50; Jeremiah 16:19; 2 Corinthians 4:16-18; 1 Thessalonians 1:5-6; Hebrews 11:25; James 5:11; Romans 8:18; Philippians 3:9-10; 1 Peter 4:14.

Personal Affirmation: I will face these afflictions with faith. I know that God will see me through. With His help, I will patiently endure all afflictions and sufferings, realizing that a far-better day lies ahead.

Meditation: *"Radical obedience to Christ is not easy. . . . It's not comfort, not health, not wealth, and not prosperity in this world. Radical obedience to Christ risks losing all these things. But in the end, such risk finds its reward in Christ. And He is more than enough for us"* (David Platt).

4
ANOINTING

Now know I that the Lord saveth his anointed;
he will hear him from his holy heaven with the
saving strength of his right hand. Some trust in
chariots, and some in horses: but we will remember
the name of the Lord. (Psalm 20:6-7)

Central Focus: The Anointed One lives within me, and His anointing breaks every yoke in my life. My God has anointed me, and His power keeps me and enables me to help others.

A Promise From God: "But the anointing which ye have received of him abideth in you, and ye need not that any man teach you: but as the same anointing teacheth you of all things, and is truth, and is no lie, and even as it has taught you, ye shall abide in him" (1 John 2:27).

Prayer: Father-God, I thank you for saving me, showing mercy to me, and always being my saving strength. Thank you for anointing me with the oil of gladness. I ask you to anoint me with fresh oil as I pray.

Your precious Spirit is upon me, Lord. Thank you for anointing me to preach good tidings unto the meek and to bind up the broken-hearted. Help me to proclaim liberty to the captives and to proclaim your acceptable year, O Lord. Enable me to comfort all who mourn and to give unto them the oil of your joy for mourning and the garment of praise for the spirit of heaviness.

All of your promises are yes and amen in Christ Jesus unto your glory, Father. Thank you for establishing me in Christ and anointing me. I love righteousness and I hate iniquity. I thank you so much for anointing me with the oil of gladness and joy.

You are ever with me, Father. Your rod and your staff bring great comfort to me. Thank you for preparing a table before me in the presence of my enemies. Thank you for anointing my head with oil. My cup overflows! Surely goodness and mercy will follow me all the days of my life, and I shall dwell in your house forever. Hallelujah!

Thank you for your promise to destroy every yoke through the power of your anointing and for removing all burdens from me.

I want your anointing to abide within me at all times, Father, and to flow forth from me to others. Because of your powerful anointing, I have no need for anyone to teach me, for your anointing teaches me about all things. Your anointing is truth, and it leads me to understand that I shall ever abide in you, Lord God.

I rejoice in your anointing, Father. Thank you so much for its power in my life.

Scriptures: Psalm 20:6-7; Psalm 28:8; Psalm 45:7; Psalm 92:10; Isaiah 61:1-3; 2 Corinthians 1:20-21; Psalm 23:5-6; Isaiah 10:27; 1 John 2:27.

Personal Affirmation: God has anointed my head with the oil of the Holy Spirit. I am His, and His power dwells within me. I will let His anointing teach me and guide me, and I will ever abide in Him.

Meditation: *"Faith does not eliminate questions. But faith knows where to take them"* (Elisabeth Elliot).

5

ANXIETY

Be careful for nothing; but in everything by prayer and supplication with thanksgiving, let your requests be made known unto God. And the peace of God, which passeth all understanding, shall keep your hearts and minds through Christ Jesus.
(Philippians 4:6-7)

Central Focus: Anxiety and worry show a lack of trust. It is far better to trust God than to spend time in anxiety and fear. I will trust the Lord with all my heart and not lean upon my own understanding. In all my ways I will acknowledge Him, and I know He will help me, direct me, and give me His peace. (See Proverbs 3:5-6.)

A Promise From God: "Casting all your care upon him; for he careth for you" (1 Peter 5:7).

Prayer: Heavenly Father, I ask in Jesus' name for your peace which surpasses all understanding, for I know that your peace will guard my heart and my mind through Christ Jesus. Therefore, I will not be anxious about anything. Instead, I will be thankful and I will let my requests be made known unto you. Thank you for your wonderful promises to me.

I humble myself under your mighty hand, Father, as I cast all my cares upon you. Thank you so much for taking care of me.

Thank you for your promise to keep me in perfect peace as I learn to stay my mind upon you, Lord. I will ever trust in you, for in you I find everlasting strength. Thank you for giving your peace to me. Because of your peace, I will not let my heart be troubled or afraid.

You have justified me, Lord God, by faith, and this brings great peace to my heart though my Lord and Savior, Jesus Christ, by whom I have access into your grace. This truth causes me to rejoice in hope of your glory and enables me to glory in tribulations, knowing that tribulation works patience, experience, and hope within me. Thank you, Father.

Your hope keeps me from being ashamed. Thank you for your love which is shed abroad in my heart by the Holy Ghost, which you've given to me. You are the God of hope, and you are filling me with all joy and peace in believing so that I would abound in hope through the power of the Holy Spirit. These truths keep me from all anxiety. Thank you, Lord.

Father, I will let your peace rule in my heart. I am so thankful for your peace, which keeps all anxiety away from me. Through your grace I will let the word of Christ dwell in me richly in all wisdom, and whatever I do in word or deed I will do all in the name of the Lord Jesus, giving thanks to you, Father, by Him.

Thank you, great God of peace, for sanctifying me wholly. I know you will preserve my whole spirit, soul, and body blameless unto the coming of the Lord Jesus Christ. Hallelujah!

Father, thank you for bringing again from the dead my Lord Jesus, that great Shepherd of the sheep, through the blood of the everlasting covenant. I ask that you will help me to be perfect in every good work to do your will. Through your power I will never be anxious again.

Thank you so much for setting me free from all anxiety, fear, and worry, Father. Your perfect love casts out all fear from my life. Glory to your mighty name.

In Jesus' peaceful name I pray, Amen.

Scriptures: Philippians 4:6-7; 1 Peter 5:7; Isaiah 26:3-4; Romans 5:1-5; Romans 15:13; Colossians 3:15-17; 1 Thessalonians 5:23; Hebrews 13:20-21; 1 John 4:18.

Personal Affirmation: I will never be anxious again, because I know that God has given me His peace and rest. His love has removed all fear from my life, and He is guarding my heart and mind through Christ Jesus.

Meditation: "*Worrying is arrogant because God knows what He's doing*" (Barbara Cameron).

6
ARMOR OF GOD

Put on the whole armour of God, that ye may be able to stand against the wiles of the devil
(Ephesians 6:11)

Central Focus: God's armor provides me with all I need for spiritual protection for every day. It guards my heart, my mind, and my spirit.

A Promise From God: "But thou, O Lord, art a shield for me; my glory, and the lifter up of mine head" (Psalm 3:3).

Prayer: Help me, Father, to be strong in you and in the power of your might. Help me to remember to put on your whole armor every day so that I would be able to stand against the wiles of the devil.

I know that I do not wrestle against flesh and blood, but against principalities, powers, the rulers of the darkness of this world, and spiritual wickedness in high places. With this is mind, I take your whole armor unto me, that I would be able to stand in the evil day and having done all, to stand.

I will stand, therefore, having my loins girt about with truth and wearing the breastplate of righteousness. My feet are shod with the gospel of peace. Thank you, Father.

I take up the shield of faith with which I will be able to

quench all the fiery darts of the wicked. Thank you for the helmet of salvation which protects my mind. Thank you for my powerful weapon—the Word of God, which is the sword of the Spirit.

Thank you for the power of prayer. I will pray always with supplication in the Spirit, watching thereunto with all perseverance and supplication for all saints.

The night is far spent, and the day is at hand. Therefore, I will cast off the works of darkness, and I will put on the armor of light you've given to me. Help me to walk honestly, as in the day, not in rioting, drunkenness, chambering, wantonness, strife, and envying. Instead, I will put on the Lord Jesus Christ, and I will make no provision for my flesh, to fulfill its lusts.

Strengthen my heart, Father, as I learn to wait on you. I will be of good courage and I will wait on you. Strengthen me according to your Word, as I put on the armor you've provided for me. I will love you, O Lord, my strength.

You are my rock, my fortress, my deliverer, my God, and my strength. I will ever trust in you. Thank you for being my buckler and my high tower. I will call upon you, for you are worthy to be praised, and so shall I be saved from my enemies. Thank you, Father, for protecting me.

Thank you for girding me with strength and making my way perfect. You have made my feet like the feet of a hind, and you have set me upon high places. Thank you for teaching my hands to war, so that a bow of steel can be broken by my arms. You have given me the shield of your salvation, and your right hand has held me up. Thank you for your gentleness, Father, for it is a great source of strength in my life.

Lord God, I know that you are alive. Blessed are you, my rock. May you ever be exalted. Thank you for avenging me and subduing all my enemies. Thank you for delivering me and lifting me up above my enemies.

Thank you for your protective armor. I will ever give thanks to you, O Lord, and I will sing praises to your name. Praise your holy name.

In Jesus, Amen.

Scriptures: Ephesians 6:10-18; Romans 13:12-14; Psalm 27:14; Psalm 119:28; Psalm 18:1-2; Psalm 18:32-35; Psalm 18:46-50.

Personal Affirmation: I will put on every piece of God's armor every day. I will be strong in the Lord and in the power of His might. Through Him and His armor I shall prevail.

Meditation: *"True faith means holding nothing back. It means putting every hope in God's fidelity to His promises"* (Francis Chan).

～∞～

7

ASSURANCE

And the work of righteousness shall be peace; and the effect of righteousness quietness and assurance forever. (Isaiah 32:17)

Central Focus: The Bible assures me of God's love for me and eternal life in Him. Nothing can perturb this assurance. I am so greatly blessed!

A Promise From God: "Let us draw near with a true heart in full assurance of faith, having our hearts sprinkled from an evil conscience, and our bodies washed with pure water" (Hebrews 10:22).

Prayer: O Father, I thank you so much for the work of righteousness in my life, which provides me with peace, quietness, and assurance forever. Thank you for allowing me to abide in the peaceable habitation you've provided for me. Thank you for giving me a sure dwelling and a quiet resting place.

Thank you for raising Jesus from the dead and the wonderful sense of assurance this gives to me. Thank you for my fellow-believers. May my heart be knit together with them in love and unto all riches of the full assurance of understanding, to the acknowledgment of your mystery.

Thank you for Jesus in whom are hid all the treasures of wisdom and knowledge. His gospel has come to me in power and in the Holy Ghost, and in much assurance. Thank you, Father. It is my desire, Father, to show great diligence to the full assurance of hope unto the end.

Help me to be a true follower of those who, through faith and patience, inherited your promises.

Thank you for giving me the boldness to enter into the holiest by the blood of Jesus, by a new and living way, which you have consecrated for me. Because I know Jesus is my High Priest, I know that I can now draw near to you with a true heart in full assurance of faith, having my heart sprinkled from an evil conscience.

Therefore, I will hold fast the profession of my faith without wavering. Father, you are so faithful to me, and I stand upon the promises you've given me through your Word. You have assured me of your peace and love, and I am very grateful for these blessings in my life.

Through your grace I will continue in the things which you have taught me. I am assured of your truth, Father, and I thank you for teaching me so much through your Word and your Spirit. Your Word has made me wise unto salvation through the faith you've imparted to me through Jesus.

Thank you for your Word, Father. It is my source of assurance. I know it was given by you, and it is profitable for doctrine, reproof, correction, and instruction in righteousness, that I would be made perfect, thoroughly furnished unto all good works. Hallelujah!

In the name of my Savior I pray, Amen.

Scriptures: Isaiah 32:17-18; Acts 17:31; Colossians 2:2-3; 1 Thessalonians 1:5; Hebrews 6:11-12; Hebrews 10:19-23; Jeremiah 14:13; 2 Timothy 3:14-17.

Personal Affirmation: In Christ, I am assured of so many things, including salvation, abundant life, peace, grace, mercy, and love, and I will walk in this assurance each day of my life. It's a blessed assurance to know that Jesus is mine!

Meditation: *"Unconditional love is an illogical notion, but such a great and powerful one"* (A. J. Jacobs).

8

BLESSINGS

The blessing of the Lord, it maketh rich, and he addeth no sorrow with it. (Proverbs 10:22)

Central Focus: God has blessed me, is blessing me, and always will bless me. In response to His blessing, I will serve Him with diligence and with joy. Paul wrote, "Blessed be the God and Father of our Lord Jesus Christ, who hath blessed us with all spiritual blessings in heavenly places in Christ" (Ephesians 1:3).

A Promise From God: "Blessings are upon the head of the just: but violence covereth the mouth of the wicked" (Proverbs 10:6).

Prayer: Thank you, Father, for already blessing me with every spiritual blessing. Thank you that your blessing prospers me, and you add no sorrow with it. Help me to be of one mind with my fellow-believers and to have compassion on others, to love as a brother or sister, and to be courteous. I never want to render evil for evil. Instead, I want to bless others. Thank you for blessing me with the ability to do so, Father.

Teach me to obey you at all times and to hearken diligently unto your voice. I thank you so much for your promise that your blessings will come on me and overtake me if I hearken to your voice and obey you. Help me to do so at all times, Father.

I rejoice in your promise that you will bless me in the city and in the field. I praise you for your promise to bless the fruit of my body and the fruit of my field. I know you will bless both my basket and my store. Thank you, Lord.

Because of your promise I will be blessed when I come in and when I go out. You will smite my enemies, and you will command your blessing upon my storehouses and upon all that I set my hand to do. Thank you for blessing me in the land that you have given to me.

Thank you, Father, for promising to establish me. Help me to keep your commandments always. Your blessings are upon me, and I am so thankful for them. Help me, Lord, to be a faithful person; thank you for your promise that I will abound with blessings. (Indeed, I already do! Praise your holy name!)

I put all my trust in you, Lord, and this enables me to be greatly blessed. As I make you my trust, I know you will always bless me. Thank you, Father. I realize, Lord, that the key to blessing in my life is to follow your ways, and I choose to do so.

I will hear your instruction and be wise. I will never refuse your teaching. Let me learn to hear your voice and to watch daily at your gates. Thank you for enabling me to find you, for in so doing, I have found real life and I have obtained your favor. Thank you, Father.

Praise you, Lord, for all the blessings you've showered upon me.

In the blessed name of Jesus I pray, Amen.

Scriptures: Ephesians 1:3; Proverbs 10:22; 1 Peter 3:8–9; Deuteronomy 28:1–9; Proverbs 10:6; Psalm 2:12; Psalm 40:14; Proverbs 8:32–35.

Personal Affirmation: From this point forward I will obey the Lord and count my blessings. I will focus on my many blessings instead of any difficulties that might occur. I will praise the name of my Lord forever and ever.

Meditation: *"We never grow closer to God when we just live life. It takes deliberate pursuit and attentiveness"* (Francis Chan).

9
BLOOD OF JESUS

*In whom we have redemption through his blood,
the forgiveness of sins, according to the riches of
his grace; wherein he hath abounded toward us in
all wisdom and prudence.* (Ephesians 1:7-8)

Central Focus: The blood of Jesus Christ cleanses us from all sin—past, present, and future. Through His blood we are made clean, we are forgiven, and we have the power to defeat the enemy.

A Promise From God: "Forasmuch as ye know that ye were not redeemed with corruptible things, as silver and gold, from your vain conversation received by tradition from your fathers; but with the precious blood of Christ, as of a lamb without blemish and without spot" (1 Peter 1:18-19).

Prayer: O God, my heavenly Father, thank you for sending Jesus to die on the cross for me. His precious blood has redeemed me and forgiven me of my sins. Help me never to forget the power of the blood of Jesus.

Thank you for enabling me to draw near to you through the blood of Jesus, my Savior and Lord. He is my peace. I know, Lord, that I was not redeemed by corruptible things, but by the blood of the Savior, as a lamb without spot or wrinkle or any such thing.

Thank you, Father, for giving me fullness of joy. I rejoice in you! Help me to walk in the light as you are in the light. In this way I will have fellowship with other believers and with you. How I praise you, Lord, that the blood of Jesus Christ cleanses me from all sin.

Thank you for justifying me freely by your grace through the redemption that is found only in Jesus Christ, whom you have set forth to be a propitiation for my sins through faith in His blood, to declare His righteousness for the remission of sins that are past, through your forbearance, dear Father.

Thank you, O God of peace, for bringing again from the dead my Lord Jesus, that great Shepherd of the sheep, through the blood of the everlasting covenant. Make me, I ask, perfect in every good work to do your will. Work in me, Lord, that which is well-pleasing in your sight, through Jesus Christ, to whom be glory forever and ever.

Thank you for the communion I have with you through the blood of Jesus Christ. Father, thank you so much for making me meet to be a partaker of the inheritance of the saints in light. Thank you for delivering me from the power of darkness and translating me into the kingdom of your dear Son. It is in Him that I have redemption through His blood, even the forgiveness of my sins.

Jesus is your image, Father, and He is the firstborn of every creature, for by Him all things were created, and He is before all things, and by Him all things consist. He is the head of the Body, your church. He is the beginning, the firstborn from the dead. May He have preeminence in all things in my life.

Thank you, Father, for letting all fullness dwell in Him, and for making peace through the blood of His cross. By Him you have reconciled all things to yourself. Thank you for the power of the blood of Jesus Christ, which is at work in my life every day.

In Jesus, Amen.

Scriptures: Ephesians 1:7-8; Ephesians 2:13-14; 1 Peter 1:18-19; 1 John 1:7-9; Romans 3:24-25; Hebrews 13:20-21; 1 Corinthians 10:16; Colossians 1:13-20.

Personal Affirmation: I am so thankful for the blood of Jesus Christ. I will let the power of His blood keep on doing its work in me, through me, and to me. I will daily wash in the blood of Jesus.

Meditation: *"Although believers by nature are far from God and children of wrath, even as others, yet it is amazing to think how nigh they are brought to Him again by the blood of Jesus Christ"* (George Whitefield).

10
BURDENS

Cast thy burden upon the Lord, and he shall sustain thee: He shall never suffer the righteous to be moved. (Psalm 55:22)

Central Focus: God is the great burden-bearer. He takes our burdens and replaces them with peace. There is no reason to ever feel burdened when we are walking with Him.

A Promise From God: "Bear ye one another's burdens, and so fulfill the law of Christ" (Galatians 6:2).

Prayer: Heavenly Father, thank you so much for your invitation for me to cast all my burdens upon you. I do so now with the full confidence that you will sustain me. Praise your holy name! I love you so much and I love your Son, the Lord Jesus Christ, who said, "Come unto me, all ye that labour and are heavy laden, and I will give you rest. Take my yoke upon you, and learn of me; for I am meek and lowly in heart: and ye shall find rest unto your souls. For my yoke is easy, and my burden is light." Yes, Lord. Thank you for the rest you've given to me.

I cast all my cares upon you, Lord, for I know how deeply you care about me. Thank you for your promise to supply all my needs according to your riches in glory by Christ Jesus. I do so now, and I know you have removed every burden from me.

O Lord, you are a shield for me. You are my glory and the lifter of my head. When I cry unto you, I know you hear me. When I lie down to sleep, I do so peacefully, for I know you have sustained me. You are so great, Lord. You heal the broken in heart and you bind up their wounds.

You are of great power, Lord, and your understanding is infinite. Thank you for understanding me and my needs and for lifting my burdens from me. I sing unto you with great thanksgiving, and I sing praises unto you.

Through your grace I will stand fast in the liberty wherewith Christ has made me free. I will not ever be entangled again with the enemy's yoke of bondage. Thank you for setting me free. Your truth has made me free.

Show me how to bear the burdens of others, Lord, for I know that as I do so, I am fulfilling the law of Christ.

Help me to live and walk in the Spirit, Father, for I know He will always be there to help me and comfort me.

In Jesus' name I pray, Amen.

Scriptures: Psalm 55:22; Matthew 11:28-30; 1 Peter 5:7; Philippians 4:19; Psalm 3:3-5; Psalm 147:6; Galatians 5:1; Galatians 5:25; John 8:32; Galatians 6:2.

Personal Affirmation: God is my great burden-bearer. I will cast all my cares upon Him, and, as I do so, I will not be anxious about anything. Jesus has invited me to come to Him and to take His yoke upon me. This will be what I do each day, because I know His yoke is easy and His burden is light.

Meditation: *"No one is useless in this world who lightens the burdens of another"* (Charles Dickens).

11
CHARACTER

That ye may be blameless and harmless, the sons of God, without rebuke, in the midst of a crooked and perverse nation, among whom ye shine as lights in the world. (Philippians 2:15)

Central Focus: The Christian character consists of many different attributes, including the following: contrition, devotion, faithfulness, truthfulness, humility, righteousness, generosity, mercy, obedience, prudence, steadfastness, sincerity, love, and watchfulness. God is building my character with these powerful building blocks.

A Promise From God: "Put on therefore, as the elect of God, holy and beloved, bowels of mercies, kindness, humbleness of mind, meekness, longsuffering; forbearing one another, and forgiving one another, if any man have a quarrel against any: even as Christ forgave you, so also do ye. And above all these things put on the bond of perfectness. And let the peace of God rule in your hearts, to the which also ye are called in one body; and be ye thankful" (Colossians 3:12-15).

Prayer: O God, I ask that you would help me to become more like you. Teach me to be always attentive to your voice, to be blameless and harmless, to be bold, and contrite. It is my desire to have a character that is Christ-like, devout, and faithful at all times.

I respect you, Father. I want to fear you at all times. Help me to follow Christ each step of my way and to give Him the preeminence in every aspect of my life. Help me to continue in the faith, Father, grounded and settled and never to be moved away from the hope of the gospel.

Help me to be a godly person who always seeks first your kingdom and your righteousness. As I do so, I know you will add all other things unto me. Thank you, Father. Keep me from all falsehood. It is my desire to be holy as you are holy, Lord.

As I pray, I put on, as one of your elect, bowels of mercy, kindness, humility, meekness, and longsuffering. Help me to forbear with others and to forgive others. Keep me humble, Lord, as I hunger for your righteousness. May I always be just in my dealings with others.

It is an adventure to be led by your Spirit, Father, and I want to follow Him always. Teach me to be generous with others. Help me to be loving, meek, and merciful toward others. Thank you for making me a new creation in Christ Jesus.

It is my desire to obey you at all times, to be prudent and pure in heart, and to remain steadfast and immoveable. I always want to abound in your work, Lord, forasmuch as I know that my labors are never in vain when they are done in and through you.

May my character development always be based on your Word and your teaching, as I endeavor to be watchful and zealous of good works. My heart's desire, Lord, is to be your follower. With your help I will walk in love, as Christ has loved me and has given himself as an offering and a sacrifice to you.

Thank you, Father, for helping me develop a character that is pleasing to you.

In Jesus' name I pray, Amen.

Scriptures: John 10:3–4; Philippians 2:15; Proverbs 28:1; Isaiah 57:15; Acts 8:2; Revelation 17:14; Malachi 3:16; John 10:4; Colossians 1:18; Colossians 1:25; Psalm 4:3; Matthew 6:33; John 1:47; Colossians 3:12; Colossians 3:12–13; Psalm 34:2; Matthew 5:6; Luke 2:25; Romans 8;14; Isaiah 32:8; Colossians 1:4; Isaiah 29:19; Psalm 37:26; 2 Corinthians 5:17; Romans 16:19; Matthew 5:13; Matthew 5:8; Luke 12:37; Titus 2:14; Ephesians 5:1-2;

Personal Affirmation: I will walk in God's love, truth, victory, and faithfulness. I will let Him mold and shape my life so that His character will come forth in all that I say and do.

Meditation: *"You can easily judge the character of a man by how he treats those who can do nothing for him"* (James D. Miles).

Choices

Choose you this day whom ye will serve.
(Joshua 24:15)

Central Focus: God has blessed us with the power of choice so that we would choose to serve Him. May all our choices glorify Him.

A Promise From God: "And if it seem evil unto you to serve the Lord, choose you this day whom ye will serve; whether the gods which your fathers served that were on the other side of the flood, or the gods of the Amorites, in whose land ye dwell: but as for me and my house, we will serve the Lord" (Joshua 24:15).

Prayer: Dear heavenly Father, help me to remember to make the right choices all the time. Help me to incline my ear unto wisdom and to apply my heart to understanding. This will enable me to make the right choices every time.

Father, today I choose life, that I and my children may live, and that I will love you, Lord God, listen to your voice, and hold fast to you. You are my life, and I praise you for always being there for me and mine. As for me and my household, we will serve you.

Thank you for Jesus who chose me and ordained me, that I would go and bring forth fruit. Help me to be a fruit-bearing Christian, Father, and let my fruit remain. I know that whatever I ask of you in Jesus' name you will do. Thank you so much for the power of answered prayer.

Thank you for choosing me out of the world. Your Word tells me, "But God hath chosen the foolish things of the world to confound the wise; and God hath chosen the weak things of the world to confound the things which are mighty." Lord, though I am foolish and weak, I thank you for choosing me. I will ever serve you.

Blessed are you, and blessed is the Lord Jesus Christ. Thank you for blessing me with all spiritual blessings in the heavenly places in Christ who chose me before the foundation of the world, that I should be holy and without blame before Him in love. Thank you for choosing me and for allowing me to choose to follow you.

Thank you, Father, for choosing me to receive your salvation through Christ and the sanctification of the Spirit and belief of the truth. Thank you for calling me. Therefore, I will stand fast in you. I am so greatly blessed to receive your love, your everlasting consolation, and your good hope. Comfort my heart, Father, and establish me in every good work and word.

Thank you for choosing me to be a soldier of the Lord Jesus Christ. Help me to be a good soldier in His service, Father. Thank you so much for helping me to be rich in faith, an heir of the kingdom which you have promised to those who love you. I love you so much, Father.

Thank you for making me into a lively stone and a spiritual house, Father. I am a part of your royal priesthood, and I offer up to you spiritual sacrifices, which are acceptable unto you by Jesus Christ. You are the Lord of lords and the King of kings. I choose to praise you forever, because you have called me and chosen me. Help me ever to be faithful to you.

In the name of Jesus I pray, Amen.

Scriptures: Proverbs 2:2; Deuteronomy 30:19; Joshua 24:15; John 15:16; John 15:19; 1 Corinthians 1:27; Ephesians 1:3–4; 2 Thessalonians 2:13; 2 Thessalonians 2:15–17; 2 Timothy 2:3–4; James 2:5; 1 Peter 2:5; Revelation 17:14.

Personal Affirmation: I choose to serve the Lord Jesus Christ. It is my honor to be His servant, ambassador, and witness. I choose to spend time alone with Him each day.

Meditation: *"It is our choices that show what we truly are, far more than our abilities"* (Joanne Kathleen Rowling).

13
COMMITMENT

*Commit thy works unto the Lord, and thy thoughts
shall be established.* (Proverbs 16:3)

Central Focus: God's Word of truth leads me to
commit my life, my ways, my works, and everything
to Him. As I do so, all things in my life change in
positive ways.

A Promise From God: "Commit thy way unto the Lord;
trust also in him; and he shall bring it to pass, and he
shall bring forth thy righteousness as the light, and thy
judgment as the noonday. Rest in the Lord, and wait
patiently for him" (Psalm 37:5-7).

Prayer: Dear Father, sanctify me through your truth.
Your Word is truth, and it is a lamp unto my feet and a
light unto my path. I am so thankful for your truth and
your Word, and I commit my life to walking in them
each step of my way. Hallelujah!

Lord, I trust in you. It is my desire to always do good.
In so doing, I know I will dwell in the land and be
fed. I delight myself in you, and you are giving me the
desires of my heart. Praise you, Father. As I commit
my way to you and trust in you, I know you will give
answers to my prayers and you will bring forth my
righteousness as the light.

I choose to rest in you, Lord, and to wait patiently for

you. I will not fret or worry about anyone or anything. With your help, I will cease from anger and forsake wrath. Through your grace, Father, I will keep that which has been committed to my trust, avoiding profane and vain babblings and the opposition of science.

Thank you for showing me that I have no reason to ever be ashamed, for I know whom I have believed, and I am persuaded that you are able to keep that which I've committed unto you against that day. Therefore, I will hold fast the form of sound words in the faith and love which I have in Christ Jesus.

Father, I commit my life to you afresh. Thank you for calling me and for sending Jesus to suffer for me, leaving me an example that I should follow in His steps. Help me to always do so, Lord. I want to be like Him, for He did no sin and He never spoke guileful words. When He was reviled, He did not revile. When He suffered, He did not threaten. Instead, He committed himself to Him that judges righteously. I commit myself to the righteous Judge as well.

In Jesus' name I pray, Amen.

Scriptures: John 17:17; Psalm 119:107; Psalm 37:3-8; 1 Timothy 6:20; 2 Timothy 1:12-13; 1 Peter 2:21-24.

Personal Affirmation: I commit my life to the Lord. He will teach me His ways so that His ways will become my ways. My thoughts become clear because I now have purpose, and all my works I commit to Him.

Meditation: *"It was character that got us out of bed, commitment that moved us into action, and discipline that enabled us to follow through"* (Zig Ziglar).

14
COMPASSION

But thou, O Lord, art a God full of compassion, and gracious, longsuffering, and plenteous in mercy and truth. O turn unto me, and have mercy upon me; give thy strength unto thy servant.
(Psalm 86:15-16)

Central Focus: God is full of compassion and mercy, and He wants us to be so filled as well. We must let His compassion flow through us to others. This will bring about change in our families, our society, and our world.

A Promise From God: "Finally, be ye all of one mind, having compassion one of another, love as brethren, be pitiful, be courteous: not rendering evil for evil, or railing for railing: but contrariwise blessing; knowing that ye are thereunto called, that ye should inherit a blessing" (1 Peter 3:8-9).

Prayer: O Lord, you are full of compassion. You are so gracious, patient, and plenteous in mercy and truth. Turn unto me and have mercy upon me. Give me your strength. Thank you, Father. Thank you so much for giving me your mercy and having compassion upon me. Show me how to be compassionate in all my dealings with others.

Thank you for forgiving all my iniquities. Your works are so great, O Lord. Your work is honorable and glorious, and your righteousness endures forever. I will remember your wonderful works and the truth that you are gracious and full of compassion. Thank you, Father.

I highly respect you, Lord God, and I take delight in your commandments. Thank you so much for your promise that your seed shall be mighty upon the Earth and the generation of the upright shall be blessed. I thank you for your promise that wealth and riches shall be in my house and your righteousness shall endure forever. Thank you for your light that shines in the darkness.

You are so gracious, full of compassion, and righteous. I want to be like you, Father. Help me to show favor and generosity toward others, and to handle my affairs with discretion. I want your compassion to flow through me, Lord.

I will speak of the glorious honor of your majesty and your wonderful works. I want to follow your example, Father, and to be gracious and full of compassion; I want to be slow to anger and of great mercy like you are. Thank you for being so good. Your tender mercies are over all your works.

All your works shall praise you, Lord, and your saints will bless you. I praise you and bless you now, dear Father. I shall speak of the glory of your kingdom and I will talk of your power. Help me to make your mighty acts known to others and to proclaim the majesty of your kingdom, which is an everlasting kingdom. Thank you for upholding me when I fall.

Help me to be united to my fellow-believers. Help me to ever have compassion upon them, to love them as family, and to be full of compassion toward them. May I never render evil for evil. Instead, show me how to be a blessing toward all others. I know you've called me to be a blessing, Father, and in so doing I know you will bless me. Thank you so much.

It is my desire to abide in you, Lord, for I know this will keep me from sin. Keep me from all deception, Father. Help me to always be righteous and compassionate, as you are righteous and compassionate. Thank you, Lord.

Through your grace I will build myself up in your love, continually looking for the mercy of the Lord Jesus Christ unto eternal life. I will make a difference by practicing compassion as the need for it arises.

Now, unto you, Father, I come with gratitude, knowing that you are able to keep me from falling and to present me faultless before your presence with exceeding joy. You are the only wise God and you are my Savior. Unto you be glory, majesty, dominion, and power both now and ever.

In the Savior's name, Amen.

Scriptures: Psalm 86:15-16; Deuteronomy 13:17; Psalm 78:38; Psalm 111:2-4; Psalm 112:1-5; Psalm 145:6-14; 1 Peter 3:8-9; 1 John 3:6-7; Jude 22-25.

Personal Affirmation: God in His mercy has been compassionate toward me. Knowing this enables me to feel compassion. I will, therefore, be compassionate, merciful, and longsuffering to others.

Meditation: *"Compassion is the basis of all morality"*
(Arthur Schopenhauer).

15

CONFESSION

If we confess our sins, he is faithful and just to forgive us our sins, and to cleanse us from all unrighteousness. (1 John 1:9)

Central Focus: God's remedy for sin is simply to confess it to Him with an attitude of repentance in our hearts as we do so. He will always be faithful to forgive our sins and to cleanse us from all unrighteousness. The blood of Jesus Christ cleanses us from all sin—past, present, and future. We also need to confess with our mouths that Jesus Christ is Lord to the glory of God, the Father.

A Promise From God: "That if thou shalt confess with thy mouth the Lord Jesus, and shalt believe in thine heart that God hath raised him from the dead, thou shalt be saved. For with the heart man believeth unto righteousness; and with the mouth confession is made unto salvation" (Romans 10:9-10).

Prayer: Father-God, I thank you for the power of confession. I confess Christ as my Savior and Lord. Help me to follow Jesus' example at all times.

I look forward to the time when every knee shall bow to you, Lord, and every tongue will confess to you. Each one of us, Father, shall have to give an account to you.

Thank you for Jesus. You have highly exalted Him and given Him a name which is above every name, that at

His name every knee should bow of things in Heaven, things on Earth, and things under the Earth. Every tongue will one day confess that Jesus Christ is Lord to your glory, Father.

Help me to remember to confess my faults to others and to pray for others. Thank you so much for your promise that the effectual, fervent prayer of a righteous man avails much. May I always pray fervently and effectually through your Holy Spirit and your Word.

I confess my sins to you, Lord, and I know that you hear me and are cleansing me from all unrighteousness. Hallelujah! Thank you for dwelling within me, Lord, and for perfecting your love within me. Thank you for giving me your Holy Spirit. Thank you for sending Jesus to be the Savior of the world. Help me always to confess Him before others and to let them know that Jesus is your Son.

Help me not to believe every spirit, Lord, but to test the spirits and see whether they are of you, because there are many false prophets in the world. Thank you for showing me how to know your Spirit, for every spirit that confesses that Jesus Christ is come in the flesh is of you, but those that do not confess Him are from the antichrist. I know I am of you, Father, and through you I have overcome all false spirits, because greater is He who is within me than he who is in the world.

Thank you for the power of confession in my life. I will always confess Jesus as my Savior and Lord. I will confess my sins. I will confess that Jesus rose from the dead. In so doing, I know that the words of my mouth shall always have great power. Thank you, Father.

In Jesus' name, Amen.

Scriptures: Matthew 10:32; Romans 10:9-10; Romans 14:11-12; Philippians 2:9-11; James 5:16; 1 John 1:9; 1 John 4:12-16; 1 John 4:1-4.

Personal Affirmation: I confess the Lord Jesus. I confess my sins. I walk in the Lord's path of righteousness because I have accepted His promise to cleanse me and save me.

Meditation: "Confession is confirmed by the heart, confessed by the tongue, and acted upon by the body" (Anonymous).

16
CONFIDENCE

It is better to trust in the Lord than to put confidence in man. It is better to trust in the Lord than to put confidence in princes. (Psalm 118:8–9)

Central Focus: Confidence stems from faith, and it builds as we get to know the Lord better. Confidence in Him is a form of trust, and trust involves clinging to the Lord at all times. Confidence in Him gives us strength and power.

A Promise From God: "But Christ as a son over his own house; whose house are we, if we hold fast the confidence and the rejoicing of the hope firm unto the end" (Hebrews 3:6).

Prayer: Abba–Father, you are my confidence, and I know you will keep me. Thank you for your strength and your keeping power in my life. Help me to find your wisdom, Lord, for I know it will give me great confidence. Thank you for your fountain of life, Father, which comes from fearing and honoring you. It enables me to depart from the snares of death. Thank you so much.

In returning and rest I shall be saved, and in quietness and in confidence I will find your strength. Thank you, Father. In Christ Jesus I have boldness and access with confidence by His faith. For me to live is Christ and to die is gain.

Help me never to have confidence in the flesh, Father. I count all things but loss for the excellency of the knowledge of Christ Jesus, my Lord. May I ever be found in Him, not having my own righteousness, which is of the Law, but that which is through the faith of Christ, the righteousness which is of you by faith.

I want to know Jesus, the power of His resurrection, and the fellowship of His sufferings. I want to be made conformable unto His death. If by any means I might attain unto the resurrection of the dead. My confidence comes from Him. Forgetting those things which are behind and reaching forth unto those things which are before, I press toward the mark for the prize of the high calling of God in Christ Jesus.

Help me to hold fast the confidence and the rejoicing of the hope I have in you until the end. Thank you for making me a partaker of Christ, as I hold fast to the beginning of my confidence steadfast until the end.

It is with confidence that I come before your throne of grace, Father, that I may find grace and mercy to help in my time of need. Thank you for the power of prayer. With your help I will never cast away my confidence, which has great recompense of reward. Thank you, Lord. Through your grace I will abide in Christ, that, when He shall appear I will have confidence and not be ashamed at His coming.

Because my heart does not condemn me, I have great confidence in you, Father. This confidence leads me to know that I will receive what I ask of you, as I keep your commandments and do those things that are pleasing in your sight. Help me ever to do so, Lord.

Father, this is the confidence that I have in you, that, if I ask anything according to your will, you hear me. Hallelujah! And because I know you hear me, I know I will have the petitions that I put before you and desire of you.

This is great confidence, Father, and I thank you for it.

In the name of Jesus I pray, Amen.

Scriptures: Proverbs 3:26; Proverbs 3:13; Proverbs 14:26; Isaiah 30:15; Ephesians 3:12; Philippians 1:21; Philippians 3:9-14; Hebrews 3:6; Hebrews 3:14; Hebrews 4:16; Hebrews 10:35; 1 John 2:28; 1 John 3:20-22; 1 John 5:14-15.

Personal Affirmation: My confidence is in the Lord. I rejoice because, as I cling to the Lord, my confidence and trust in Him grows.

Meditation: *"With confidence, you can reach truly amazing heights; without confidence, even the simplest accomplishments are beyond your grasp"* (Unknown).

17

CONTENTMENT

But godliness with contentment is great gain. (1 Timothy 6:6)

Central Focus: Knowing God and living for Him is the source of all true contentment.

A Promise From God: "Let your conversation be without covetousness; and be content with such things as ye have: for he hath said, I will never leave thee, nor forsake thee" (Hebrews 12:5).

Prayer: Heavenly Father, thank you for showing me that godliness with contentment is great gain for me. I brought nothing into this world, and I realize that I can take nothing out. Help me to be content with what you give to me.

Thank you for supplying all my need according to your riches in glory by Christ Jesus. Help me to always be content regardless of the circumstances I'm up against. Show me the secret of being content in any and every situation.

Thank you for the happiness I have in you and for the cheerful heart you've given to me. It truly is like a continual feast for me. Help me to remember that a cheerful heart is good medicine. I understand that finding satisfaction in the work you give to me brings contentment to my heart.

I wait patiently for you, Lord, and I still my heart before you. I do not fret over wicked men who apparently succeed in their ways. I will eat my food with gladness and drink with a joyful heart, because I know you have extended your favor to me.

I will keep myself free from the love of money, which is the root of all evil. Through your grace I will be content with what I have. I am so grateful, Father, for the truth of your promise that you will never leave me nor forsake me. Hallelujah!

Thank you for your peace that surpasses all understanding. Because of your peace, which guards my heart and my mind, I will not be anxious about anything. Instead, I will let my requests be made known unto you, Father, and I will meditate upon whatsoever things are honest, just, pure, lovely, and of good report.

You are the God of peace, and I know you are always with me. Thank you, Father. I can do all things through Christ who strengthens me. You are the portion of my inheritance, and you maintain my lot. Thank you for the goodly heritage you've given to me. I will bless you, O Lord. Thank your for your counsel in my life.

I have set you always before me. Because you are at my right hand, I know I shall not be moved . Therefore, my heart is glad and I am content. My glory rejoices in you and my flesh rests in the hope you've given to me.

Thank you for showing me the path of life. In your presence there is fullness of joy and contentment. At your right hand there are pleasures forevermore.

Help me to walk in contentment every day of my life.

In Jesus' name, Amen.

Scriptures: 1 Timothy 6:6-8; Philippians 4:19; Philippians 4:11-12; Proverbs 15:13; Proverbs 15:15; Proverbs 17:22; Ecclesiastes 2:24; Psalm 37:7; Ecclesiastes 9:7; Hebrews 13:5; Philippians 4:6-13; Psalm 16.

Personal Affirmation: I am content with all the Lord has given me.

Meditation: *"Contentment is a pearl of great price, and whoever procures it at the expense of ten thousand desires makes a wise and a happy purchase"* (John Balguy).

18

DECISION-MAKING

I call heaven and earth to record this day
against you, that I have set before you life and
death, blessing and cursing: therefore choose
life, that both thou and thy seed may live.
(Deuteronomy 30:19)

Central Focus: Go to God before making any decision. Open His Word, and ask Him to direct your steps. Pray to the Father who knows what you need even before you express it to Him.

A Promise From God: "Choose you this day whom ye will serve . . . . but as for me and my house, we will serve the Lord" (Joshua 24:15).

Prayer: Father–God, help me always to remember to seek first your kingdom and your righteousness, realizing that as I do this, you will add everything else I need to me. Teach me your way, O Lord, and I will walk in your truth. Give me an undivided heart, that I may always fear your name.

Teach me, O Lord, to follow your decrees. With your help, I will keep them to the end. Give me understanding, and I will keep and obey your law with all my heart. Direct me in the path of your commands, for it is in them that I find my delight. Turn my heart toward your statutes and not to selfish gain.

You are my portion, O Lord. I have promised to obey your words. I am your servant. Give me discernment that I may understand your statutes. I will call you, O Lord. Answer me, for I want to obey all your decrees.

With your help, Father, I will pursue righteousness, godliness, faith, love, endurance, and gentleness. Enable me to fight the good fight of faith, as I take hold of the eternal life to which I've been called. Help me to keep your commands without spot or blame until the appearing of the Lord Jesus Christ.

Help me to prepare my mind for action and to be self-controlled. I set my hope fully on the grace that will be given to me when Jesus Christ is revealed. I am eager to make my calling and my election sure, realizing that this will keep me from falling.

I choose to remain in you, Lord, and I know you will remain in me. I realize that no branch can bear fruit by itself; it must remain in the vine in order to do so. Thank you, Lord. I will remain in you, and I know I shall bear much fruit. You are the vine; I am but a branch. Apart from you I can do nothing.

Just as I have received Christ Jesus as my Lord, I will continue to live in Him. I choose to be rooted and built up in Him, strengthened in the faith as I was taught. My heart truly overflows with thankfulness and gratitude to you for making all these things possible.

Help me to stand firm and hold to your teaching. Thank you for encouraging my heart and strengthening me in every good deed and word. Help me to grow in the grace and knowledge of my Lord and Savior, Jesus Christ. To Him be glory both now and forever!

In His name I pray, Amen.

Scriptures: Matthew 6:33; Psalm 86:11; Psalm 119:33; Psalm 119: 57; Psalm 119:125; Psalm 119:145; 1 Timothy 6:11; 1 Peter 1:13; 2 Peter 1:10; John 15:4–5; Colossians 2:6; 2 Thessalonians 2:15; 2 Thessalonians 2:17; 2 Peter 3:17.

Personal Affirmation: I have already chosen that I will come to the Lord whenever I have a decision to make. I choose to serve the Lord. I choose life.

Meditation: *"Choices are the hinges of destiny"* (Edwin Markham).

19

DILIGENCE

*But without faith it is impossible to please him;
for He that cometh to God must believe that he is,
and that he is a rewarder of them that diligently
seek him.* (Hebrews 11:6)

Central Focus: Diligence involves dedication, perseverance, and staying focused. It is an important part of the Christian life.

A Promise From God: "The hand of the diligent maketh rich" (Proverbs 10:4).

Prayer: Dear heavenly Father, it is my desire to be your diligent follower. Help me to be diligent in my obedience to you, for I know your promise is that if I hearken diligently to your commandments to love you and to serve you with all my heart and soul, that you will give me the first rain and the latter rain. Thank you, Father.

I choose to hearken diligently unto you. I will incline my ear to you and come to you. In so doing, I know my soul shall live and you will confirm your everlasting covenant to me. With your help, Father, I will forget those things which are behind and I will reach forth unto those things which are before. Through your grace I will press toward the mark for the prize of your high calling in Christ Jesus.

Thank you for your promises, Father, for it is by them that I shall be a partaker of your divine nature. Therefore, I will give all diligence to add virtue to my faith and knowledge to my virtue. Likewise, I will add temperance to my knowledge, patience to my temperance, godliness to my patience, brotherly kindness to my godliness, and love to my brotherly kindness.

Help me to keep my soul diligently. Help me to attend to your words, Lord, and incline my ear to your sayings. Do not let them depart from my eyes. Teach me how to keep them in the midst of my heart, for they are life to me and health to my flesh. Help me to keep my heart with all diligence, for I know that out of it are the issues of life.

I thank you, Lord, that you are not unrighteous to forget your work and labor of love. Help me to show that same diligence to the full assurance of hope unto the end. I never want to be slothful, Father, but I always want to be a follower of those who, through faith and patience, inherited your promise.

It is my desire, Lord, to be diligent at all times. I want to be found of you in peace, without spot, and blameless. I will diligently seek good, Father, and I thank you for your favor in my life. Help me never to deal with a slack hand, but always to be diligent, for I know this will lead to prosperity.

In Jesus' precious name I pray, Amen.

Scriptures: Deuteronomy 11:13-14; Isaiah 55:2-3; Philippians 3:13-14; 2 Peter 1:4-7; Deuteronomy 4:9; Proverbs 4:20-22; Hebrews 6:10-12; 2 Peter 3:14; Proverbs 11:27; Proverbs 10:4.

Personal Affirmation: With faith, I seek the Lord and follow His righteous ways. I will diligently persevere.

Meditation: *"What we hope ever to do with ease, we must first learn to do with diligence"* (Samuel Johnson).

20

ETERNAL LIFE

For God so loved the world, that he gave his only begotten Son, that whosoever believeth in him should not perish, but have everlasting life. (John 3:16)

Central Focus: The life that is to come—eternal life—is indescribably wonderful and blessed. It is a life that never ends and, by the way, it has already begun for all those who have committed their lives to Christ.

A Promise From God: "Laying up in store for themselves a good foundation against the time to come, that they may lay hold on eternal life" (1 Timothy 6:19).

Prayer: Father, you are the high and lofty one who inhabits eternity. You are holy and your name is holy. You dwell in the high and holy place. I look forward to dwelling with you forever. You are the true and living God. You are the everlasting King.

Hear, O Lord, and have mercy upon me. Be my Helper. Thank you for turning my mourning into dancing for me and for putting off my sackcloth. You have girded me with gladness. Praise your holy name. To the end that my glory may sing praise to thee and not be silent, O Lord my God. I will give thanks unto you forever.

Blessed are you, O Lord, from everlasting to everlasting. Your name shall endure forever, and I am blessed in you. Hallelujah! Lord, you have been my dwelling place in all generations. Before the mountains were brought forth and before you formed the world, from everlasting to everlasting you are God.

Hallowed be your name, Father. Your kingdom come. Your will be done on Earth as it is in Heaven. Give me this day my daily bread, and forgive my debts as I forgive my debtors. Lead me not into temptation, but deliver me from evil, for yours is the kingdom, the power, and the glory forever.

Thank you so much for giving me length of days forever and ever. Thank you for allowing me to drink of the water of life, which has become a spring of water that wells up within me to eternal life. I listen for your voice, Lord, and I follow you. Thank you for giving eternal life to me, so that I will never perish.

Eternal life involves knowing you, Lord, and I want to know you more fully. Thank you for your great gift, which is eternal life in Christ Jesus my Lord. I look forward to the time when the perishable will clothe itself with the imperishable and the mortal with immortality. I thank you for the certain knowledge that death has been swallowed up in victory.

Lord, with your help I will not let my heart be troubled. I believe in you and in your Son, the Lord Jesus Christ. Thank you for letting me know that there are many mansions in your house. Thank you for Jesus who is preparing a place for me there. I look forward to His return, so that I may be with Him forever.

In Jesus' name I pray, Amen.

Scriptures: Isaiah 57:15; Jeremiah 10:10; Psalm 31:10-12; Psalm 41:13; Psalm 72:17; Psalm 90:1-2; Matthew 6:10-13; Psalm 21:4; John 4:14; John 10:27; John 17:2; Romans 6:22; John 14:1-3.

Personal Affirmation: Everlasting life is a gift I already have because God gave His only begotten Son. I believe.

Meditation: *"I want to know one thing: the way to Heaven. God himself has condescended to teach me the way. He has written it down in a book. Oh, give me that book! At any price give me the book of God. Let me be a man of one book"* (John Wesley).

21

FAITH

But what saith it? The word is nigh thee, even in thy mouth, and in thy heart: that is, the word of faith, which we preach. (Romans 10:8)

Central Focus: The Word of God builds faith in our hearts, and we must have this faith if we want to please God. Faith enables us to appropriate God's promises into our lives.

A Promise From God: "For whatsoever is born of God overcometh the world: and this is the victory that overcometh the world, even our faith" (1 John 5:4).

Prayer: I love your Word, O Lord, and I thank you that it builds faith in my heart. The faith you impart to me helps me to be sure of what I hope for and to be certain of what I do not see. Without faith it is impossible to please you, because when I come to you I must believe that you exist and that you greatly reward everyone who seeks you. I want to please you, Father, and I thank you for the rewards you give to me through faith.

I trust the words of Jesus who said that when I believe, I will receive what I ask for in prayer. What a wonderful promise this is.

Help me, Father, to trust in you with all my heart instead of leaning upon my own understanding. In all my ways I will acknowledge you, knowing that you will continue to direct my steps. I believe in the name of your Son, Jesus Christ, and I trust His promise that everything is possible for those who believe.

By faith I eagerly await through the Spirit the righteousness for which I hope. I want to always express my faith through love, as I realize this is the most important thing in life. It is through faith that I am able to approach you with complete confidence.

I want Christ to dwell in my heart through faith, and I want to be rooted and established in love. Help me, Lord. I claim your promise that when I have faith in you I will be able to do the same things you have done, and because Jesus is now in Heaven with you I will be able to do even greater things than those. Thank you, Father.

I fix my eyes upon Jesus, who is the author and finisher of my faith. For the joy that was set before Him, He endured the cross for me, scorning its shame, and now He has sat down at your right hand. Hallelujah!

By faith I will stand firm, and I will take up the shield of faith by which I will be able to quench all the fiery darts of the wicked one. Help me, Lord, to continue always in the faith, established and firm, and not moved away from the hope of the gospel.

Help me to be rooted and built up in Christ. Strengthen me in the faith, which is of far greater worth than gold, which perishes even though it is refined by fire. May my faith be proved genuine and may it result in praise, glory, and honor when Jesus Christ is revealed.

Though I have not seen Him, I love Him. Though I do not see Him now, I believe in Him and I am filled with an inexpressible and glorious joy, as I receive the goal of my faith, which is the salvation of my soul. Thank you for showing me that the victory that overcomes the world is faith.

I pray in Jesus' faithful name, Amen.

Scriptures: Hebrews 11:1; Hebrews 11:6; Mark 11:23-24; Proverbs 3:5-6; 1 John 3:23; Mark 9:29; Galatians 5:5; Ephesians 3:12; Ephesians 3:17; John 14:12; Hebrews 12:2; 2 Corinthians 1:24; Colossians 1:23; Hebrews 10:22; 1 Peter 1:7; 1 John 5:4.

Personal Affirmation: Because I trust Jesus and believe in God, I have faith, which is the evidence of things not seen.

Meditation: *"The only saving faith is that which casts itself on God for life or death"* (Martin Luther).

22
FAITHFULNESS

O love the Lord, all ye his saints: for the Lord
preserveth the faithful, and plentifully rewardeth
the proud doer. Be of good courage, and he shall
strengthen your heart, all ye that hope in the Lord.
(Psalm 31:23–24)

Central Focus: In Proverbs we read, "Many a man claims to have unfailing love, but a faithful man who can find?" (Proverbs 20:6). Faithfulness is a virtue and to walk in faithfulness requires total abandonment to Christ.

A Promise From God: "A faithful man shall abound with blessings" (Proverbs 28:20).

Prayer: O heavenly Father, I come to you now in faith, realizing how much I need to be a more faithful person in all that I say, think, and do. Help me, Lord.

Thank you for your Word which tells me, "He that is faithful in that which is least is faithful also in much: and he that is unjust in the least is unjust also in much." Help me to be faithful in the small things as well as the big things.

Fill me afresh with your Spirit, Father, that I would produce His fruit in all the relationships and responsibilities of my life. One very important fruit of your Spirit is faithfulness, and I realize that if I am going to be faithful, I must be filled with your Holy Spirit. Help me to walk in your Spirit each step of my way.

I love you, Lord. Thank you for preserving me. Show me how to always be of good courage. Strengthen my heart, as I place all my hope in you. As I learn to walk in faithfulness, I know I shall abound with blessings, Father. Thank you so much for your faithfulness to me.

Through your strength I will endure until the end. Thank you for your faithful love, which casts all fear from my life; it keeps me from being afraid of what I might have to face or suffer. Help me to be faithful, Father, even to the point of death.

As I persevere in faithfulness, I know that one day I will hear you say to me, "Well done, good and faithful servant! You have been faithful with a few things; I will put you in charge of many things. Come and share your Master's happiness!"

You have given me a special trust, Father, and I realize that my response should be to show my faithfulness to you. I want to be like you, Lord, and you are always faithful. You are my Rock. Your works are perfect, and all your ways are just. You are my faithful God who never does wrong. Upright and just are you.

I will sing of your great love forever. With my mouth I will make known your faithfulness throughout all generations. I will declare that your love stands firm forever and that you have established your faithfulness in Heaven.

In the faithful name of Jesus I pray, Amen.

Scriptures: Luke 16:10; Galatians 5:22; Psalm 31:23–24; Proverbs 28:20; Matthew 10:22; Revelation 2:10; Matthew 25:23; 1 Corinthians 4:2; Deuteronomy 32:4; Psalm 89:1.

Personal Affirmation: I will continue to live in faithfulness with all my being.

Meditation: *"Faithfulness is not doing something right once but doing something right over and over and over"* (Joyce Meyer).

23
FAMILY

For this cause shall a man leave his father and mother, and shall be joined unto his wife, and they two shall be one. (Ephesians 5:31)

Central Focus: Many families today are being destroyed for a lack of spiritual knowledge. God instituted the family to be the cornerstone of society. It is so important to follow His plan for marriage and the family. Let us pray for our families.

A Promise From God: "Believe on the Lord Jesus Christ, and thou shalt be saved, and thy house" (Acts 16:31).

Prayer: O God, my heavenly Father, I thank you for my family and I ask you to bless us with every blessing in Christ Jesus. Help me to manage my own family well and to see that my children obey me with proper respect.

Help me to train up my children in the way that they should go, realizing that when they are old they will not depart from your ways. Through your grace I will be careful to lead a blameless life and to walk in my house with a blameless heart.

Help me to teach your ways to the members of my household both by precept and example. May I never forget to talk about your ways and your Word whenever I am with my family—when I sit at home, when I walk along the road with them, when I lie down, and when I get up. I will pray for my family every day, knowing that you hear me and answer my prayers. Hallelujah!

As for me and my household, we will serve you, O Lord. Help us to live under you in unity. Help us to live in forgiveness and mutual forbearance. I want to teach your Word to my family, Father. Help us ever to rejoice together under you.

May no member of my family ever depart from you. Thank you for your blessing in our lives. Teach us to walk in all your ways. May the woman of our household be as a fruitful vine, and may the children of my household be like olive plants around our table.

Bless us, Lord. May I live to see my children's children and to see peace upon the Earth. Help me to manage the affairs of our household wisely, and may we ever worship you together. Father, I believe in you, so I ask that my whole household would be saved.

Help our family to be a good example of family life to the world, to be like the families of Jacob, Joshua, David, Job, Lazarus of Bethany, Cornelius, Lydia, the Philippian jailer, Crispus, and Lois. Give us your wisdom, Father, as we build our family, and help us ever to remember that unless you build the house, those who build it labor in vain.

I will sing of mercy and judgment, Lord. Unto you I will sing. Help me to always be a good example to the members of my family. Through your grace I will set no wicked thing before my eyes. Hear my prayer, O Lord, and let my cry come unto thee.

Thank you for your mercy, which is from everlasting to everlasting and your righteousness is upon me and my children and my grandchildren. Help us to keep your commandments. I trust you to keep any evil from ever coming to my family.

In Jesus' name I pray, Amen.

Scriptures: Ephesians 1:3; 1 Timothy 3:4; Proverbs 22:6; Psalm 101:2; Deuteronomy 11:19; Psalm 83:1; Joshua 23:15; Psalm 133:1; Matthew 18:21-22; Deuteronomy 4:9-10; Deuteronomy 14:26; Psalm 128; Proverbs 31:27; Proverbs 14:1; Psalm 101:1-3; Psalm 102:1-2; Psalm 103:17; Psalm 91:10.

Personal Affirmation: Because I am a child of God, I am a member of God's family. I will be led by the Lord and will lead my family—my spouse, my children and grandchildren, my own siblings—in God's ways.

Meditation: *"A family is a place where principles are hammered and honed on the anvil of everyday living"* (Chuck Swindoll).

24
FEAR OF GOD

The fear of the Lord is the instruction of wisdom;
and before honour is humility. (Proverbs 15:33)

Central Focus: To fear God is to respect, honor, reverence, and adore Him. It is also to fear stepping away from Him, because to do so would mean to step outside of His presence, the source of peace, joy, and pleasures forevermore.

A Promise From the Father: "O fear the Lord, ye his saints: for there is no want to them that fear him" (Psalm 34:9).

Prayer: Mighty God, I come to you with respect and honor because I know who you are and how important you are to me. As I learn to fear you, I gain wisdom and spiritual understanding. Fearing you helps me to hate evil, and it adds years to my life. Thank you, Father. It is a fountain of life to me.

Through love and faithfulness sin is atoned for, and through fearing you I am enabled to avoid evil. Thank you, Father. Continue to give me singleness of heart and action, so I will always fear you both for me and my children. Thank you for making an everlasting covenant with me. I know you will never stop doing good to me, and I will never turn away from you.

Thank you for your promise to confide in me as I fear

you. Make your covenant known to me, O Lord. Thank you for your angels, which are encamping around me as I fear you. Thank you for delivering me. You have told me that as I fear you, I will lack nothing. Hallelujah!

Thank you for your love, Father, which is so great—as high as the heavens are above the Earth. Thank you for the compassion you have for me. You are my Father, and I know you love me very much. Your love for me is from everlasting to everlasting, and your righteousness will be imparted to me, my children, and their children. Bless your name for this promise, Lord.

Thank you for your promise of wealth, honor, and life to all who fear you. Thank you for showing me that fearing you gives me your power, providence, justice, and forgiveness.

I will ever fear you, Father, and I will serve you. Help me to hold fast to you at all times. May I always fear you and serve you faithfully with all my heart. I will never forget all the great things you have done for me.

How great is your goodness, O God, which you have stored up for those who fear you, which you bestow in the sight of men on those who take refuge in you. I fear you, Father, and I take refuge in you. You alone are to be feared.

Teach me your way, O Lord, and I will walk in your truth. Give me an undivided heart, that I may fear your name. I will praise you, O Lord my God, with all my heart, and I will glorify your name forevermore. Your mercy toward me is great, and you have delivered my soul. You are a God who is full of compassion, and you are gracious, longsuffering, and plenteous in mercy and truth.

O turn to me, and have mercy upon me. Give your strength to me, your servant. Thank you for helping me and comforting me at all times.

In Jesus' name I pray, Amen.

Scriptures: Psalm 111:10; Proverbs 8:13; Proverbs 10:27; Psalm 14:27; Proverbs 16:6; Jeremiah 32:39; Psalm 25:12; Psalm 34:7; Psalm 34:9; Psalm 103:11; Psalm 103:17; Proverbs 22:4; Jeremiah 5:22; 1 Samuel 12:2-4; Job 37:19-24; Psalm 130:4; Deuteronomy 10:20; 1 Samuel 12:24; Psalm 31:19; Psalm 76:7; Psalm 86:11-17.

Meditation: *"Shame arises from the fear of men, conscience from the fear of God"* (Samuel Johnson).

25

FELLOWSHIP

That which we have seen and heard declare we unto you, that ye also may have fellowship with us: and truly our fellowship is with the Father, and with his Son Jesus Christ. (1 John 1:3)

Central Focus: God wants to have fellowship with us, and He wants us to have fellowship with other believers as well. Fellowship involves intimate communion, understanding, compassion, and the bearing of one another's burdens.

A Promise From God: "And to make all men see what is the fellowship of the mystery, which from the beginning of the world hath been hid in God, who created all things by Jesus Christ" (Ephesians 3:9).

Prayer: Thank you, Father, for showing me that two are better than one, because they have a good return for their work. A cord of three strands is not easily broken. Praise your name, Lord. Help me to walk in agreement with my fellow-believers.

I believe your promise, Lord, that if two of us shall agree as touching anything that they shall ask, it shall be done for them by my heavenly Father. Hallelujah!

Father, you created me to have fellowship with you. Show me what I need to do in order to have fellowship with you. It is great to know that I'm a member of your body, Lord. Help your people to be like those in the Book of Acts on the Day of Pentecost—they were all together in one place, and they devoted themselves to the apostles' teaching and to fellowship, to the breaking of bread and prayer.

Repair the divisions within the Body of Christ, Father, I pray. Lead me into fellowship with the Holy Spirit. I have received tremendous encouragement from being united with Christ and great comfort from His love. Help me to share those qualities with others in fellowship.

Lord, I want to make your joy complete by being like-minded with other believers. May I never do anything out of ambition or vain conceit, but in humility I want to consider others as being better than myself.

Encourage me within my heart, Father, and unite me with others in love, so that I and my fellow-believers may have the full riches of complete understanding and know your mysteries. Help me to bear with the failings of the weak, and not just to please myself. Help me to build others up in the faith.

I look forward to the time, Father, when we engage in a spirit of unity among ourselves as we follow Jesus Christ and we will glorify you with one heart and mouth. Help me to bear the burdens of others and thereby fulfill the law of Christ.

Thank you, Father, for the grace of the Lord Jesus Christ, and your love, and the fellowship of the Holy

Spirit. May I ever walk in your grace, love, and the fellowship of the Holy Spirit.

In Jesus' name, Amen.

Scriptures: Ecclesiastes 4:9; Ecclesiastes 4:12; Amos 3:3; Matthew 18:19; Acts 1:14; Acts 2:1; Acts 2:42; Philippians 2:1-3; Colossians 2:3; Romans 15:1; Galatians 6:2; 2 Corinthians 13:14.

Personal Affirmation: I am so comfortable when I fellowship with other believers because I feel I am at home with family. I fellowship with the Lord by praying and reading His word.

Meditation: *"Our love to God is measured by our everyday fellowship with others and the love it displays"* (Andrew Murray).

26
GIFTS FROM GOD

According as his divine power hath given unto us all things that pertain unto life and godliness, through the knowledge of him that hath called us to glory and virtue. (2 Peter 1:3)

Central Focus: God is the Giver of every good and perfect gift. (See James 1:17.) He supplies all our need according to His riches in glory by Christ Jesus. (See Philippians 4:19.)

A Promise From God: "Every good and perfect gift is from above, and cometh down from the Father of lights, with whom is no variableness, neither shadow of turning" (James 1:17).

Prayer: O God, my heavenly Father, thank you for all the gifts you've given to me. Thank you for the Lord Jesus Christ who saved me. Thank you for the Holy Spirit, who provides me with so much. He is my Comforter.

Thank you for providing me with material blessings, such as food, drink, shelter, and clothing. Thank you for the beauty of your creation. Thank you, Lord, for wisdom and for peace.

You have filled my heart with great joy, Father, and your joy is my strength. Thank you for the strength and power you've given to me. Help me to please you at all times, Father, so that I will receive your gifts of wisdom, knowledge, and happiness.

I ask that you would continue to reveal deep and hidden things to me. Through Christ I have been enriched in every way. Because of Him I do not lack any spiritual gifts, as I await the coming of my Lord Jesus Christ.

Thank you for giving me the desires of my heart and the requests of my lips. I believe the promise of your Word, Father, which tells me that those who seek you will lack no good thing. I believe this with all my heart.

Thank you, also, for being my sun and my shield and for bestowing favor and honor upon me. Help me to keep my walk blameless, Father. I know you will withhold no good thing from me. Praise your holy name!

Give me an undivided heart, Lord, and put a new spirit within me. Give me a heart of flesh instead of a stony heart. Thank you for making my joy complete by answering my prayers. You are so gracious to me, Father, and you give me so many wonderful things. Hallelujah!

I put all my hope in you, Lord, and I know you will provide everything I need for my life, including enjoyment. Every good and perfect gift comes from you, Father, and I praise you that you do not change like shifting shadows.

Blessed be you, the God and Father of my Lord Jesus Christ, for you have blessed me with every spiritual blessing in heavenly places in Christ. Thank you, Lord.

Give me the spirit of wisdom and revelation in the knowledge of Christ. Enlighten the eyes of my understanding, that I will surely know the hope of your calling and the riches of the glory of your inheritance in the saints.

Thank you for giving me a measure of your grace according to the measure of the gift of Christ. Thank you for giving me your whole armor, which enables me to withstand in the evil day.

Thank you for enabling me to be strong in you and in the power of your might.

In Jesus' name I pray, Amen.

Scriptures: John 4:10; John 14:16; Matthew 6:25, 33; Psalm 19:1; Proverbs 4:7; John 14:27; Psalm 29:11; Nehemiah 8:10; Ecclesiastes 2:26; Daniel 2:21; Matthew 25:14-20; Psalm 21:2; Psalm 84:11; Ezekiel 11:19; John 16:23; Romans 8:32; Ephesians 1:3; Ephesians 1:18; Ephesians 4:7; Ephesians 6:13.

Personal Affirmation: When I use the gifts God gave me I feel fulfilled and happy. It is a pleasure, and it brings me great joy, to use my gifts in God's service and to help others.

Meditation: *"What we are is God's gift to us. What we become is our gift to God"* (Eleanor Powell).

27
GRACE

But grow in grace, and in the knowledge of our Lord Jesus Christ. To him be glory both now and forever. (2 Peter 3:18)

Central Focus: God's grace enables us to be what we could not be, to do what we could not do, and to receive what we could not receive.

A Promise From God: "For by grace are ye saved through faith; and that not of yourselves; it is the gift of God: not of works, lest any many should boast" (Ephesians 3:8–9).

Prayer: Father of grace and glory, I thank you for the grace you've imparted to my heart. It was your grace that brought salvation to me, and I will never forget the moment when Jesus came into my heart and set me free. Thank you, Lord.

You have poured out your love and your grace upon me so abundantly, Father, along with the faith and love that are in Christ Jesus. Thank you so much for your grace and love.

You have given me life and you have shown me kindness. In your providence you have watched over me. Thank you for your grace which is at work in my life. When anxiety was great within me, your consolation and your grace brought joy to my soul.

No temptation has seized me except that which is common to others. You are so faithful, Father, and I know your grace will not permit me to be tempted beyond what I can bear. I know you will provide me with a way out so that I will be able to keep standing. Hallelujah!

I go forth from glory to glory and from strength to strength. Thank you so much for your grace which enables me to do so.

I am very confident that you will carry on to completion the work you have begun in me. This is your grace at work in my life, and I am so thankful for it. May my love abound more and more in knowledge and in depth of insight. Keep me pure and blameless until the day of Jesus Christ, filled with the fruit of righteousness that comes through Jesus Christ—to your glory and praise.

Help me, Father, to live a life that is worthy of the Lord. I want to please Him in every way, bearing fruit in every good work and growing in the knowledge of you. Strengthen me with all power according to your glorious might so that I will have great endurance, patience, and joy.

May my love increase and overflow to others. Strengthen my heart so that I will be found blameless and holy in your presence, Father, when Jesus returns. I look forward to that day. Thank you, Father, for predestinating me to be adopted as your child through Jesus Christ, in accordance with His pleasure and will—to the praise of His glorious grace, which He has freely given to me in the One He loves.

In Him I have redemption through His blood, the forgiveness of sins, in accordance with the riches of your grace that you lavished on me with all wisdom and understanding. Thank you for making known to me the mystery of your will, according to your good pleasure, which you purposed in Christ.

In the name of Jesus I pray, Amen.

Scriptures: Romans 6:23; Ephesians 6:23; 1 Timothy 1:14; Psalm 94:7; 1 Corinthians 10:13; Philippians 1:9; Colossians 1:10; 1 Thessalonians 3:12; Ephesians 1:5.

Personal Affirmation: All the good things in my life, including my relationship with the Lord, have come by God's grace. When I think of other paths I might have taken, I often reflect, "There, but for the grace of God, go I" (attributed to John Bradshaw). I thank God for the grace He has provided.

Meditation: *"Twas grace that taught my heart to fear and grace my fears relieved. How precious did that grace appear the hour I first believed"* (John Newton).

28
HAPPINESS

How excellent is thy lovingkindness, O God!
Therefore the children of men put their trust under
the shadow of thy wings. They shall be abundantly
satisfied with the fatness of thy house; and thou
shalt make them drink of the river of thy pleasures.
(Psalm 36:7-8)

Central Focus: True happiness comes from knowing Jesus and living for Him. Another word for "happiness" is "blessedness." We are blessed, and God's blessings make us happy.

A Promise From God: "Happy is the man that findeth wisdom, and the man that getteth understanding" (Proverbs 3:13).

Prayer: Father, thank you for the happiness I have as a result of knowing you and your Son, my Lord Jesus Christ. I always want to please you, Lord, for I know you will give me wisdom, knowledge, and happiness as a result.

Help me to dwell in unity with my fellow-believers, because I know this will give me happiness. Help me to give to the needy and not to hold back, for I know this leads me into blessedness. Thank you, Father. I always want to be a cheerful giver.

Thank you for putting gladness in my heart, Father. I will

both lie down in peace and sleep, for you make me to dwell in safety. Your throne, O God, is forever and ever. Your kingdom is a scepter of righteousness. I love your righteousness, and I thank you for anointing me with the oil of gladness and happiness.

Thank you for ransoming me, Lord, from the enemy's clutches. Thank you for putting songs and everlasting joy upon my head. I praise you for the joy, gladness, and happiness you've given to me. I know that all sorrow and sighing shall flee away from me.

I will bless you, O Lord, for giving me counsel. I have set you always before me, and because you are always at my right hand, I know I shall not be moved. Praise your name! Therefore, my heart is glad and my glory rejoices. My flesh shall rest in hope.

Thank you for showing me the path of life. In your presence there is fullness of joy, and at your right hand there are pleasures forevermore. Thank you, Father, for the happiness this brings to me. Thank you for turning my captivity and for filling my mouth with laughter and my tongue with singing.

You have done so many great things for me, and as I contemplate on these blessings, my heart is gladdened. Turn again my captivity, O God, as the streams in the south. Help me to ever remember that those who sow in tears shall reap in joy.

Let me bear precious seed as I go forth. I will come again rejoicing, bringing many sheaves with me. Hallelujah!

Father, with your help I will endure until the end, for I know this will bring great happiness to both me and you. May I never forget that your joy is my strength.

Scriptures: Ecclesiastes 2:24; Psalm 133:1; Psalm 14:21; 2 Corinthians 9:7; Psalm 4:7-8; Hebrews 1:8-9; Isaiah 35:10; Proverbs 16:7-11; Psalm 126:3-6; James 5:11; Nehemiah 8:10.

Personal Affirmation: All the good things in my life, including my relationship with the Lord, have come by God's grace. When I think of other paths I might have taken, I often reflect, "There, but for the grace of God, go I" (attributed to John Bradshaw). I thank God for the grace He has provided.

Meditation: *"For every minute you are angry you lose sixty seconds of happiness"* (Ralph Waldo Emerson).

29

HEALING

*If thou wilt diligently hearken to the voice of the
Lord thy God, and wilt do that which is right in
his sight, and wilt give ear to his commandments,
and keep all his statutes, I will put none of these
diseases upon thee. . . . for I am the Lord that
healeth thee (Exodus 15:26)*

Central Focus: All healing comes from God. When you
are sick, try to determine what caused it and by what
means God wants to bring healing to you.

A Promise From God: "If thou wilt diligently hearken
to the voice of the Lord thy God, and wilt do that
which is right in his sight, and wilt give ear to his
commandments, and keep all his statutes, I will put
none of these diseases upon thee, which I have brought
upon the Egyptians: for I am the Lord that healeth
thee" (Exodus 15:26).

Prayer: O God, my heavenly Father, you are my healer
and I trust you with all my heart. During this illness I will
not lean upon my own understanding. Instead, in all
my ways I will acknowledge you, and I know you will
direct me to find answers to my needs.

I know you heal in answer to my prayer of faith, so I present
my need for healing to you. I know you hear and answer
my prayers. Thank you, Father. With your help I will obey
your commandments and abide by your statutes.

Jesus healed all manner of sickness and disease, and I thank you for all the wonderful examples in your Word of His healing power. He healed a disabled man, a woman with an issue of blood, lepers, Peter's mother-in-law, those who were paralyzed, a man with a withered hand, people who were blind, and those who were mute. He truly is the Great Physician, and I look fully to Him for the healing I need.

Thank you for promising health to me. I know that fearing you, Lord, brings health to my body. Your Spirit, who raised Christ from the dead, dwells in me, and I know He is quickening my mortal body. Thank you, Father, for Jesus and the Holy Spirit.

I receive the promises of your Word, Father, which tell me that I am more than a conqueror through Jesus who loves me. I am fully persuaded that nothing shall be able to separate me from your love, not death, life, angels, principalities, powers, present things, things to come, height, depth, nor any creature, including sickness. Thank you for your love, which I know so fully through Jesus Christ, my Lord, and thank you for His healing power which is at work in my life.

I will ever make you my refuge, Lord, and you, the Most High, shall ever be my habitation. Thank you for your angels, which you've given charge over me, to keep me in all my ways. I praise you for your promise that no evil will befall me and no plague will come near my dwelling.

As I set my love upon you, Lord God, I thank you for

delivering me from this illness. Thank you for helping me rise above it and for answering my prayers when I call unto you. I claim your promise that you will be with me in trouble. I know you are delivering me and honoring me.

Thank you for your promise to give me long life. Indeed, you are fully satisfying me, Father, and you are showing me the completion of your salvation. Praise your mighty name!

In the name of Christ who is my Healer I pray, Amen.

Scriptures: Exodus 15:26; Proverbs 3:5-6; Exodus 15:26; John 5:2-9; Matthew 9:20-22; Mark 1:40-45; Matthew 8:14-15; Luke 6:6-10; Matthew 9:27-33; Matthew 8:17; Exodus 15:26; Proverbs 3:7-8; Romans 8:11; Romans 8:37-39.

Personal Affirmation: I praise God and I offer up my illness or my condition in prayer for healing. When I am ill, I reflect on the relationship that often exists between my physical condition and my spiritual condition. God wants to heal me both spiritually and physically, and I want to allow Him to. I want to do that which is right in His sight.

Meditation: *"We must avoid all ambiguities particularly when it comes to our health. One way of maintaining your health is to be joyful, happy, and thankful. These attitudes are better than any medicine, I can assure you"* (Dr. Phillip Goldfedder, M.D.).

30
HEAVEN

In my Father's house are many mansions: if it were not so, I would have told you. I go to prepare a place for you. (John 14:2)

Central Focus: This world is not your home, but Heaven is! Are your treasures laid up in Heaven or upon Earth? God's gift to you is eternal life through His Son, our Lord Jesus Christ.

A Promise From God: "For the hope which is laid up for you in heaven, whereof ye heard before in the word of truth of the gospel" (Colossians 1:5).

Prayer: Eternal Lord, I thank you for establishing your throne in Heaven, and I look forward to being there with you at the appointed time. I lift up my eyes to you. Help me not to be quick with my mouth or hasty in my heart to utter anything before you. You are in Heaven. I am upon Earth, and I want my words to be few.

Your Word tells me that you are the high and lofty One and that you inhabit eternity. It also declares that you live with those who are contrite and lowly in spirit. Help me to be humble and contrite, Father. It thrills me to know that Heaven is your throne and the Earth is your footstool. I lift up my heart and my hands to you, Lord.

My Father in Heaven, hallowed be your name. Your kingdom come. Your will be done on Earth as it is in

Heaven. Give me this day my daily bread and forgive me of my sins, as I forgive others. Lead me not into temptation and deliver me from evil. For yours is the kingdom and the power and the glory forever.

I thank you for the river of the water of life which emanates from your throne in Heaven. It is clear as crystal and so refreshing and cleansing in its power. It is my heart's desire, Father, to always be one of your servants. I look forward to the time when I will see your face and your name will be on my forehead. Then there will be no more night and I will not need the light of a lamp or the light of the sun, for you will give me light, and I will reign with you forever. Thank you for this wonderful promise, Father.

Thank you, Father, that I know I have your house in Heaven. It is not made with hands, but it is eternal in the heavens. Thank you for all the promises of Heaven from whence I look for the Savior, the Lord Jesus Christ, for I know He will change my vile body into a body that is fashioned like His glorious body, according to the working whereby He is able even to subdue all things unto himself. Thank you, Father.

Thank you, Father, for making it possible for me to be a partaker of the inheritance of the saints in light and for delivering me from the power of darkness and for translating me into the kingdom of your dear Son.

One day before long I know Jesus will descend from Heaven with a shout, with the voice of the archangel, and with the trump of God. At that time the dead will rise first and those of us who remain will be caught up together with them in the clouds, to meet Him in the air. And so shall we ever be with Him. Praise your mighty name!

I know I have in Heaven a better and an enduring substance. Therefore, I will not cast away my confidence, which has great reward. Father, thank you so much for the better and heavenly country you have prepared for me. Thank you for not being ashamed to be called my Father and for preparing an eternal city for me.

Blessed are you, the God and Father of the Lord Jesus Christ. Thank you for begetting me unto a lively hope by the Resurrection of Jesus Christ from the dead to an incorruptible and undefiled inheritance that will never fade away because it is reserved in Heaven for me.

Father, help me to be an overcomer so that I may sit with you at your throne in Heaven.

In the blessed Savior's name I pray, Amen.

Scriptures: Psalm 103:19; Psalm 123:1; Ecclesiastes 5:2; Isaiah 57:15; Isaiah 66:1; Lamentations 3:41; Matthew 6:9-13; Revelation 22:1-5; 2 Corinthians 5:1; Philippians 3:20-21; Colossians 1:12-13; 1 Thessalonians 3:16-17; Hebrews 10:34-35; Hebrews 11:16; 1 Peter 1:3-5; Revelation 3:21.

Personal Affirmation: I have a taste of Heaven on Earth, but *only* a taste. How much more real, how much more substantial, how much more solid Heaven is than I can even imagine. Oh, how I look forward to spending Eternity with you in the place you have prepared for me.

Meditation: *"Earth has no sorrow that Heaven cannot heal"* (Thomas More).

31

HOLINESS

*For I am the Lord your God: ye shall therefore
sanctify yourselves, and ye shall be holy;
for I am holy.* (Leviticus 11:44)

Central Focus: Holiness is imparted to us through faith in the Holy One. Through His help we can walk in holiness and righteousness every day.

A Promise From God: "Give unto the Lord the glory due unto his name; worship the Lord in the beauty of holiness" (Psalm 29:2).

Prayer: Holy God, I want to be holy like you. I want to be holy in everything I do, because you are holy and I want to be like you. Through your grace I will make every effort to live in peace with all people and to be holy, for I know that without holiness I shall not be able to see you.

Thank you for choosing me, Lord, as one of your holy and beloved children. Help me to clothe myself with compassion, kindness, humility, gentleness, and patience. Help me to be a forgiving person and to put on love, which is the perfect bond of unity. I will let the peace of Christ rule in my heart and I will be thankful.

O God of peace, I ask that you would sanctify me thoroughly, through and through. May my entire spirit, soul, and body be kept blameless and holy at the coming of the Lord Jesus Christ. I thank you for sanctifying me through the work of the Holy Spirit and my belief in the truth.

It is my heart's desire to always pursue righteousness, holiness, faith, love, and peace along with all those who call on you out of a pure heart. Praise you, Father. With your help I will add goodness to my faith, knowledge to my goodness, self-control to my knowledge, perseverance and godliness to my self-control, brotherly kindness to my godliness, and love to my brotherly kindness.

Father, thank you for showing me that my body is the temple of the Holy Spirit, who is within me. I have received Him from you. Therefore, I am not my own; I was bought with the price of Christ's shed blood. From this point on I will honor you with my body, my soul, and my spirit.

Whether I eat or drink, no matter what I do, I want to do all for your glory, Father. Help me to put to death everything that belongs to my earthly nature: sexual immorality, impurity, lust, evil desires, and greed. I renounce all forms of idolatry in my life.

I want my life to be lived in a manner that is worthy of you, Lord. Thank you for calling me into your kingdom and glory. Strengthen my heart, that I might be blameless and holy in your presence, Father, and when my Lord returns with all His holy ones.

Your Word teaches me to say no to all ungodliness

and worldly passions. Help me to live a self-controlled, upright, and godly life in this present age. Help me always, Father, to live a godly and holy life as I look forward to the day of the Lord.

I look forward to the return of the Lord Jesus Christ, and as I do so, I will make every effort to be found spotless, blameless, and at peace with Him.

In the holy name of Jesus I pray, Amen.

Scriptures: 1 Peter 1:15; Hebrews 12:14; Colossians 3:12-15; 1 Thessalonians 5:22; 2 Thessalonians 2:13; 2 Timothy 2:21; 2 Peter 1:5; 1 Corinthians 6:19; 1 Corinthians 10:31; Colossians 3:5; 1 Thessalonians 3:13; Titus 2:13; 2 Peter 3:11; 2 Peter 3:14.

Personal Affirmation: With God's help I will live a sanctified and holy life. I want to be holy as He is holy. He commands me to be holy, and He has provided a way for me to be holy, and I have faith that He imparts holiness to me, for He has promised to do so.

Meditation: *"If you will stop here and ask yourself why you are not as pious as the primitive Christians were, your own heart will tell you that it is neither through ignorance nor inability, but because you never thoroughly intended it"* (William Law).

32
HOLY SPIRIT

But the Comforter, which is the Holy Ghost,
whom the Father will send in my name, he shall
teach you all things, and bring all things to your
remembrance, whatsoever I have said unto you.
(John 14:26)

Central Focus: The Holy Spirit will guide me into all truth, for He is the Spirit of truth. He is my Comforter and my source of power. He helps me in my weakness and teaches me how to pray.

A Promise From God: "And I will pray the Father, and he shall give you another Comforter, that he may abide with you forever; even the Spirit of truth; whom the world cannot receive, because it seeth him not, neither knoweth him; for he dwelleth with you, and shall be in you" (John 14:16–17).

Prayer: Heavenly Father, thank you for sending your Holy Spirit to help me in my daily life. I love you, and I love Him. He lives with me and will always be within me. I am so thankful that I know the Holy Spirit as my Counselor. He is teaching me all things and bringing all the teachings of your Word to my remembrance.

I ask that the Holy Spirit would convict the world of sin. May He lead men to the truth, and may He guide me into all truth as well. He encourages me every day and every moment. He gives me the power to witness effectively to others. Father, I am so grateful that you have given the Holy Spirit to me.

Help me to live according to the Spirit, not according to my sinful nature. I want to be led by your Spirit, Father, for in so doing, I show that I am your child. The Holy Spirit helps me in my weaknesses, and when I do not know how to pray or what to pray for, He leads me. Thank you for His intercession in my life, for I know He prays for me with groanings that cannot be uttered.

Thank you for saving me through the washing of rebirth and renewal by the Holy Spirit. Thank you for pouring him out upon me so generously. Sanctify me by the Holy Spirit. Thank you for choosing me, Lord, through the sanctifying work of the Spirit, for obedience to Jesus Christ and the sprinkling of His blood.

It is so wonderful to know that the same Spirit that raised Jesus from the dead now dwells in me, and He is quickening my mortal body. Thank you, Father. May the fellowship of the Holy Spirit always be with me. Thank you for giving me access to you through the Holy Spirit. Help me to pray in and through Him.

Through your grace I will remember that it is not by might nor by power, but by your Spirit that I shall prevail. Thank you, Father. Out of your glorious riches, I know you are strengthening me with power through the Holy Spirit in my inner being.

I am grateful for the liberty I experience through the Holy Spirit. I put on all the armor you've provided for me, Father, including the helmet of salvation and the sword of the Spirit, which is your Word. I believe we are living in the time that was prophesied by your prophet Joel, a time when you are pouring out your Spirit on all flesh. Thank you, Lord.

I give my life afresh to you, Father. Control me by the Holy Spirit who lives within me. May I never grieve the Holy Spirit by whom I have been sealed for the day of redemption. Thank you for your kingdom, which is not a matter of eating or drinking, but of righteousness, peace, and joy in the Holy Spirit.

Fill me with all joy and peace, Father, as I trust in you, so that I will overflow with hope by the power of the Holy Spirit.

Through Jesus Christ my Lord I pray, Amen.

Scriptures: John 14:16; John 14:26; John 16:4; Acts 9:31; Acts 1:8; Acts 15;8; Romans 8:4; Romans 8:26; Titus 3:5; Romans 15:16; 1 Peter 1:2; Romans 8:11; 2 Corinthians 13:14; Ephesians 2:18; Jude 20; Zechariah 4:6; Ephesians 3:16; 2 Corinthians 3:17; Ephesians 6; Joel 2:28; Romans 8:9; Ephesians 4:20; Romans 14:17; Romans 15:13.

Personal Affirmation: The Holy Spirit is my Comforter. Sent to me by the Father in the name of Jesus, the Holy Spirit teaches me all things and brings to my remembrance the things that Jesus has said.

Meditation: *"We must be, we must be, we must be baptized with the Holy Spirit—and refilled time and again as our service for God necessitates it"* (R. A. Torrey).

33
HOPE

For thou art my hope, O Lord God: thou art my trust from my youth. (Psalm 71:5)

Central Focus: Hope is the anchor for your soul. It is a mixture of faith, trust, and belief. Put your hope in God, not in the things of this world.

A Promise From God: "The eyes of your understanding being enlightened; that ye may know what is the hope of his calling, and what the riches of the glory of his inheritance in the saints, and what is the exceeding greatness of his power to us-ward who believe, according to the working of his mighty power" (Ephesians 1:18-19).

Prayer: God of all hope, I come to you with joy and expectation, because I hope in you. I will be strong and take heart. Let your unfailing love rest upon me, O Lord, even as I place all my hope in you. I wait for you, O Lord, and I know you will answer me. Thank you for always being there for me.

My hope is in you, and I will praise you, my Savior and my God. Because of you, I will always have hope, and I will praise you more and more. I know that with you there is unfailing love and full redemption. The hope I have in you makes me happy and blesses me. My confidence is in you, Father.

The hope of your salvation is my helmet, O God, and your faith and love are my breastplate. The hope I have from you and in you is the anchor for my soul, and it is firm and secure. I rejoice in the hope of your glory, Father, and I will remain joyful in hope, patient in affliction, and faithful in prayer. Hallelujah!

May the eyes of my heart be enlightened, Father, in order that I would know the hope to which you have called me and the riches of your glorious inheritance in the saints. Thank you for the faith and love that spring from the hope that is stored up for me in Heaven.

Keep me from ever being moved from the hope that is held out in the Gospel of Jesus Christ. He is my hope of glory! Thank you for the faith and knowledge you've imparted to me. They rest upon the hope of eternal life with you. Thank you for the promise of eternal life.

I will keep on waiting for the blessed hope—the glorious appearing of our great God and Savior, Jesus Christ. Praise be to you, O God, the Father of my Lord Jesus Christ! In your great mercy you have given me a new birth into a living hope through the Resurrection of Jesus Christ from the dead. Hallelujah!

I set my hope fully on the grace that will be given to me when Jesus Christ is revealed. The hope you've imparted to me, Father, purifies me. Thank you for sanctifying me through hope. I put my hope in your Word and its wonderful promises to me. Your Scriptures give me great hope.

O great God of hope, I ask you to fill me with all joy and peace as I trust in you, so that I may overflow with hope by the power of the Holy Spirit.

In the name of Jesus Christ I pray, Amen.

Scriptures: Psalm 31:24; Psalm 33:22; Psalm 38:15; Psalm 43:5; Psalm 146:5; Jeremiah 17:7; 1 Thessalonians 5:8; Hebrews 6:19; Romans 5:2; Romans 12:12; Ephesians 1:18; Colossians 1:5; Colossians 1:23; Colossians 1:27; Titus 1:2; Titus 2:13; 1 Peter 1:3; 1 Peter 1:13; 1 John 3:3; Psalm 119:74; Romans 15:4; Romans 15:13.

Personal Affirmation: I hope in the Lord. Therefore, I expect His promises to be fulfilled and I trust Him.

Meditation: *"There are no hopeless situations; there are only men who have grown hopeless about them"* (Claire Booth Luce).

34

HUMILITY

The fear of the Lord is the instruction of wisdom;
and before honour is humility. (Proverbs 15:33)

Central Focus: One antonym for humility is pride, and pride, one of the Seven Deadly Sins, is the downfall of so many people. Humility entails lowliness of mind, not thinking of ourselves too highly, and focusing on the needs of others instead of our own.

A Promise From God: "Humble yourselves therefore under the mighty hand of God, that he may exalt you in due time" (1 Peter 5:6).

Prayer: I humble myself before you, Father. Thank you for the wisdom you are imparting to me. Such wisdom comes through humility. Thank you for living with me, Lord, and for reviving my spirit and my heart as I learn to walk in humility. I believe you will esteem me as I learn to humble myself and walk in contrition before you and as I revere your holy Word. Thank you for all the promises of your Word.

Like Paul, may I never boast except in the cross of the Lord Jesus Christ, through which the world has been crucified to me, and I to the world. May I never praise myself with my own lips. I want to avoid selfishness in all its ugly forms.

Help me to have child-like faith, Father, and to humble

myself like a little child. Help me not to think more highly of myself than I ought to think. Instead, let me use sober judgment in thinking of myself in accordance with the measure of faith you've given to me.

Help me to be devoted to my brothers and sisters in the faith. May I always practice brotherly love and honor others above myself. Show me how to live in harmony with others, Father. May I never be proud or conceited. Help me to submit to others out of reverence for Christ.

Dear Lord, I want to be like Jesus in all that I say and do. He made himself nothing, taking the very form of a servant and made in human likeness. He humbled himself and became obedient unto death—even death on a cross! Therefore, you exalted Him to the highest place and gave Him a name that is above every name, that at the name of Jesus every knee should bow in Heaven and on Earth and under the Earth, and every tongue should confess that Jesus Christ is Lord, to your glory, Father-God.

As one of your chosen people, Father, I desire to clothe myself with compassion, kindness, humility, gentleness, and patience. Fill me afresh with your Spirit, that I would produce His fruit in all the relationships and responsibilities of my life.

As I humble myself before you, Father, I know you will lift me up. Praise your mighty name! Thank you for your promise that humility and fearing you bring wealth, honor, and life. Thank you for promising the Kingdom to those who are poor in spirit.

Not that I have already been made perfect, but I press on to take hold of that for which Christ Jesus took hold of me. This one thing I do: forgetting what is behind and pressing on to what lies ahead, I press toward the mark for the prize of the high calling of God in Christ Jesus.

In the Savior's name I pray, Amen.

Scriptures: Proverbs 11:2; Isaiah 57:15; Isaiah 66:2; Galatians 6:14; Proverbs 27:2; Matthew 18:2; Romans 12:10; Romans 12:16; Philippians 2:6–11; Colossians 3:12; Galatians 5:22; James 4:10; Proverbs 22:4; Matthew 5:3; Philippians 3:12-14.

Personal Affirmation: I humble myself before the Lord, for I have nothing to brag about other than His cross.

Meditation: *"True humility is not thinking less of yourself; it is thinking of yourself less"* (C.S. Lewis).

35

INHERITANCE

*Blessed be the God and Father of our Lord
Jesus Christ, Who hath blessed us with all
spiritual blessings in heavenly places in Christ.*
(Ephesians 1:3)

Central Focus: As Christians, we are heirs of God, and
the inheritance He gives to us is immeasurably full of
blessings, for He is the Giver of every good and perfect
gift. (See James 1:17.) We are joint-heirs with His Son,
Jesus Christ, because we have been adopted into the
family of God.

A Promise From God: "In whom also we have obtained
an inheritance, being predestinated according to the
purpose of him who worketh all things after the counsel
of his own will" (Ephesians 1:11).

Prayer: Father-God, I thank you for giving me so many
things through Christ. I am enjoying your inheritance
and I am deeply grateful for all you are giving to me.
Thank you for the Word of your grace, which builds
me up and gives me an inheritance among those who
are sanctified.

Thank you for adopting me into your family, Father.
As one of your children, I am your heir, a joint-heir
with Jesus Christ. In Him I was chosen, having been
predestinated according to your plan. Thank you for
working everything out according to the purpose of

your will. May I ever be for the praise of your glory.

Because I believed, I was marked in Him with a seal, the promised Holy Spirit. Thank you, Father, for Him—a deposit that guarantees my inheritance until the redemption of those who are God's possession—to the praise of your glory.

Thank you, Father, for justifying me according to your grace, for this enables me to be an heir who has the hope of eternal life. Praise your mighty name. Help me to diligently hearken unto your voice, O Lord. I want to be obedient to your teachings.

How it blesses me to know that you promise so many blessings to me. As I pray, I realize that your blessings are actually overtaking me. Thank you, Father. I know I will be blessed in the city and blessed in the field. I know that the fruit of my body shall be blessed, as will the fruit of my ground. My basket and my store shall be blessed as well.

I believe your Word that tells me that I will be blessed when I come in and when I go out. I claim these blessings, Father.

It is wonderful to know that another part of my inheritance is that you will cause my enemies to be smitten. Hallelujah! Thank you for commanding your blessing upon my storehouses and in everything that I set my hand to. What a wonderful inheritance this is. Thank you for blessing me in the land you've given to me.

Establish me in holiness, Father, as I endeavor to obey your commandments every day. I ask you to open unto me your good treasure and to bless all the works of my hands. I praise you for making me the head and not the tail. I shall be above only and not beneath.

Thank you for the wonderful blessings and inheritance I am enjoying as your child.

In Jesus' name I pray, Amen.

Scriptures: Acts 20:32; Romans 8:16; Ephesians 1:11; Titus 3:7; Deuteronomy 28.

Personal Affirmation: What a blessed assurance it is that I have inherited God's gifts and blessings as a joint-heir with Jesus.

Meditation: *"The unthankful heart discovers no mercies; but the thankful heart will find, in every hour, some heavenly blessings"* (Henry Ward Beecher).

36
JOY

The joy of the Lord is my strength. (Nehemiah 8:10)

Central Focus: The believer is very familiar with joy, which is a fruit of the Holy Spirit, and a dynamic source of power in our lives. As we pray, we experience the joy of the Lord, which is our strength.

A Promise From God: "Whom having not seen, ye love; in whom, though now ye see him not, yet believing, ye rejoice with joy unspeakable and full of glory" (1 Peter 1:8).

Prayer: Father, thank you for joy. You have turned my mourning into dancing and you have removed my sackcloth and clothed me with joy. Hallelujah. My heart rejoices in you, for I trust in your holy name. Help me to ever sing for joy in you.

Dear God of hope, fill me with all joy and peace as I trust in you so that I will overflow with hope by the power of the Holy Spirit. Though I have not seen you, I love you, Lord. I believe in you, and this fills me with an inexpressible and glorious joy. Thank you, Father.

Your Word is the joy of my heart. I rejoice in your promises like one who finds great spoil. Thank you, Lord. You are my salvation, Father. I will trust and not be afraid. You are my strength and song, and you have become my salvation. With joy I will draw water from your wells of salvation.

Thank you for including me in your kingdom, Lord. Your kingdom is not a matter of eating and drinking, but of righteousness, peace, and joy in the Holy Spirit. Thank you for making known to me the path of life and filling me with joy in your presence. Thank you for giving me your pleasures forevermore.

I glory in your holy name, and I greatly rejoice. Thank you for strengthening me with all power according to your glorious might so that I will have great endurance and patience and joy, as I give thanks to you, Father, for making me a partaker of the inheritance of the saints in light.

Thank you for delivering me from the power of darkness and translating me into the Kingdom of your dear Son in whom I have redemption through His blood, even the forgiveness of sins. He is your image, O God, the firstborn of every creature. By Him were all things created in Heaven and on Earth, visible and invisible. He is before all things, and by Him all things consist. Thank you for Jesus, Father, for He is the source of all my joy and rejoicing. I rejoice in Him.

You have granted so many eternal blessings to me, Father, and you have made me exceedingly glad with the joy of your presence. Thank you so much. Gladness and joy are overtaking me as I pray and experience your presence.

In the joyful name of Jesus I pray, Amen.

Scriptures: Psalm 30:11; Psalm 33:21; Psalm 132:16; Romans 15:13; 1 Peter 1:8; Psalm 119:111; Isaiah 12:2; Romans 14:17; Psalm 16:11; Psalm 105:3; Colossians 1:11–14; Psalm 21:6; Isaiah 35:10.

Personal Affirmation: The joy of the Lord is, indeed, my strength.

Meditation: *"Joy is increased by spreading it to others"* (Robert Murray McCheyne).

—∞∞∞—

37
LOVE

Beloved, let us love one another: for love is of God;
And every one that loveth is born of God, and
knoweth God. He that loveth not knoweth not God;
for God is love. (1 John 4:7-8)

Central Focus: The Supreme Commandment directs us to fully love God and others. They will know we are Christians by our love. Faith, hope, and love abide, but the greatest of these is love. (See 1 Corinthians 13:13.)

A Promise From God: "There is no fear in love; but perfect love casteth out fear: because fear hath torment. He that feareth is not made perfect in love" (1 John 4:18).

Prayer: Help me, Father, to let my love always be sincere, as I hate what is evil and cling to that which is good. I want to love my neighbor as myself, as you direct me to do. Help me to remember that love never does harm to its neighbor, for it is the fulfillment of the Law.

Teach me to live a life of love, Lord, and to do everything in love just as Christ loved me and gave himself as a fragrant offering and sacrifice to you. Let my love increase and overflow toward others, and may my love abound more and more in knowledge and depth of insight.

May the love I give out always come from a pure heart,

a good conscience, and a sincere faith. Help me to set an example for others in speech, life, love, faith, and purity. I will pursue righteousness, faith, love, and peace along with all who call on you out of a pure heart.

I want others to know that I am a disciple of the Lord Jesus Christ, and I know it is the love I exhibit that will help them to understand this. Father, I will follow the way of love, as I desire your spiritual gifts. As one of your chosen people, Lord, I will clothe myself with compassion, kindness, humility, gentleness, and patience. I will bear with others and be a forgiving person. I will put on love, which is the bond of perfection.

Show me how to love with actions and in truth, not only with words. Thank you for living within me, Father, and I know your love is made complete in me. Hallelujah! I will share your love with others.

I believe that Jesus is the Christ and so I am born of you, Father. I love you and your Son. I also love your children, and I will show forth your love by carrying out your commandments.

Though I speak with the tongues of men and of angels, and have not love, I am become as sounding brass or a tinkling cymbal. Father, help me to always remember that love suffers long and is kind, and that love does not envy. As I walk in love, I will reflect on the truth that love is not proud, does not misbehave, does not seek its own, is not easily provoked, and thinks no evil.

Your love never rejoices in iniquity, Father, but it always

rejoices in the truth. I want to rejoice in the truth at all times, Lord. With your help, I know my love will bear all things, believe all things, hope all things, and endure all things. I thank you that your love never fails.

There now abides faith, hope, and love, and I realize that the greatest of these is love. Thank you for the blessings of love, Father.

In the loving name of Jesus I pray, Amen.

Scriptures: Romans 12:9; Romans 13:8; Ephesians 5:2; 1 Thessalonians 3:12; Philippians 1:9; 1 Timothy 1:5; 1 Timothy 6:11; 1 Corinthians 14:1; Colossians 3:12; 1 John 3:16; 1 John 4:11; 1 John 5:1; 1 Corinthians 13.

Personal Affirmation: The Bible says that everyone who loves is born of God and knows God. It is because I love that I know that I am God's. I have no fear, for perfect love casts out fear.

Meditation: *"God is clearly deserving of our love especially if we consider who He is that loves us, who we are that He loves, and how much He loves us"* (Bernard of Clairvaux).

38

MIRACLES

The same came to Jesus by night, and said unto him, Rabbi, we know that thou art a teacher come from God: for no man can do these miracles that thou doest, except God be with him.
(John 3:2)

Central Focus: Our God is a miracle worker. His signs, wonders, and miracles are always amazing. Every miracle is a testament to the power of God and His love for people. The miraculous gifts of the Holy Spirit are not to be neglected or despised. Indeed, they should be sought after. (See 1 Corinthians 12:3, 1 Timothy 4:14, and 1 Thessalonians 5:20.)

A Promise From God: "God also bearing them witness, both with signs and wonders, and with divers miracles, and gifts of the Holy Ghost, according to his own will" (Hebrews 2:4).

Prayer: Miracle-working Father, I thank you for all the miracles I've seen and experienced. Your power is awesome and marvelous to behold. Thank you for the power of the Holy Spirit and all His wondrous works. May everyone who sees your miracles seek you with all their hearts.

Your miracles are such marvelous things, Father, and I rejoice that you've allowed me to see your hand at work in so many wondrous ways. So many miracles have been accomplished through the name of Jesus Christ, my Lord and Savior.

The Bible is full of reports of your miracle-working power. Thank you for revealing to me how you created the world, opened Rachel's womb, brought forth water from the rock, and healed lepers. These are only a few of the countless miracles you've performed. Thank you, Father.

Help people to believe in you when they see your miracles. As Daniel said, it is a great pleasure to tell others about the miraculous signs and wonders of the Most High God. How great are your signs, Father, and how mighty are your wonders! Your kingdom is an eternal kingdom, and your dominion endures from generation to generation.

Your wonders reveal your glory, Lord, and they cause people to believe in you. Thank you for sharing about the miracles of old in your Word. They are written so that we would believe in you. By believing in you, Lord, I have life through your name. Hallelujah!

Accomplish your miracles through me, Lord God. Lead others to a saving knowledge of Jesus through them. Thank you for all your marvelous works. You divided the Red Sea and led your people with a cloud by day and a pillar of fire by night. You split the rocks open so that your people would have water to drink, and you provided them with manna as food.

Thank you for the many miracles of the Great Physician,

Jesus. You accredited Him by miracles, wonders, and signs, which you did through Him. Thank you that He is still at work today.

In the name of the great Miracle-worker I pray, Amen.

Scriptures: Acts 17:17-18; Psalm 78:12; Acts 4:30; Genesis 1; Genesis 30:20; Exodus 17:5-7; Mark 1:40-45; Exodus 4:30-31; Daniel 4:2; John 2:11; John 20:30; Romans 15:18; Psalm 78:12-29; Acts 2:22.

Personal Affirmation: Jesus told us that all things are possible to those who believe. (See Mark 9:23.) I believe, for I have seen miracles. I may not have recognized them as miracles at the time, but upon reflection I realize what a great miracle-worker our Lord and Savior is.

Meditation: *"Miracles are a retelling in small letters of the very same story which is written across the whole world in letters too large for some of us to see"* (C.S. Lewis).

39

OBEDIENCE

And hereby we do know that we know him, if we keep his commandments. He that saith, I know him, and keepeth not his commandments, is a liar, and the truth is not in him. (1 John 2:3-4)

Central Focus: Obedience to the Lord always brings His blessings into our lives. To obey Him is to follow Him and His teachings every step of the way. As the old hymn says, "Trust and obey, for there's no other way to be happy in Jesus than to trust and obey."

A Promise From God: "Wherefore gird up the loins of your mid, be sober, and hope to the end for the grace that is to be brought unto you at the revelation of Jesus Christ; as obedient children, not fashioning yourselves according to the former lusts in your ignorance: but as he which hath called you is holy, so be ye holy in all manner of conversation" (1 Peter 1:13-15).

Prayer: Father, my delight is in your law, and on your law I will meditate both day and night. I have chosen your way of truth. I have set my heart on your laws, and I will hold fast to your statutes, O Lord. Do not let me be put to shame.

Help me to obey your laws forever, Father. Your Word is a lamp unto my feet and a light unto my path. Through your grace I will walk in the light it sheds each step of my way. My heart is set on keeping your statutes to the very end.

O Lord, it is my heart's desire to follow your commands. I will obey your statutes, for I love them greatly. I will obey your precepts and your statutes, for all my ways are known to you. Teach me to do your will, for you are my God. May the Holy Spirit always lead me.

Thank you for your love, for it leads me to walk in obedience to your commands. Help me to ever walk in your love, Father. Thank you for choosing me through the sanctifying work of the Holy Spirit, for obedience to Jesus Christ and sprinkling by His blood.

Show me how to be careful to follow every command you have given to me, so that I will live, increase, and enter the Promised Land. Teach me how to observe your commands and walk in your ways and revere you.

It is my heart's desire to carefully observe all your commands, Father. I will love you, walk in your ways, and hold fast to you. Thank you for your promise that everywhere I set my foot will be mine. Thank you for setting before me a blessing and a curse: a blessing if I obey your commands, which I want always to do, and a curse if I disobey you.

I will follow you and revere you, Lord God. Help me to always keep your commands and obey you. I will serve you and hold fast to you. Help me to follow your decrees and laws each step of my way and to carefully observe them with my heart and soul. You are the Lord, my God, and I will walk in your ways and keep your decrees, commands, and laws. I will obey you, Father. Thank you for letting me be one of your people. Indeed, you have revealed to me that I am one of your treasured possessions. Help me to keep all your commands.

In the mighty name of Jesus I pray, Amen.

Scriptures: Psalm 1:2; Psalm 119:30; Psalm 119:44; Psalm 119:105; Psalm 119:112; Psalm 119:166; Psalm 143:10; 1 Peter 1:2; Deuteronomy 8:11; Deuteronomy 11:22–27; Deuteronomy 13:4; Deuteronomy 26:16–18.

Personal Affirmation: With God's help, I trust and obey His commands. Since God has created me, He knows what is best for me. Being obedient to Him brings His blessings upon me and, with these blessings, spiritual, physical, and mental health. I have no ulterior motive but to obey God's commands out of love for what He has done for me.

Meditation: *"Wicked men obey from fear; good men, from love"* (Augustine).

40

PATIENCE

Be patient therefore, brethren, unto the coming of the Lord. Behold, the husbandman waiteth for the precious fruit of the earth, and hath long patience for it, until he receive the early and latter rain.
(James 5:7)

Central Focus: Patience is a fruit of the Holy Spirit in our lives. The trying of our faith works patience in our lives. James writes, "Let patience have her perfect work, that ye may be perfect and entire, wanting nothing" (James 1:4).

A Promise From God: "Knowing this, that the trying of your faith worketh patience. But let patience have her perfect work, that ye may be perfect and entire, wanting nothing" (James 1:3-4).

Prayer: Lord God, thank you for your love in my life. It is patient and kind, and I learn a great deal from your love. I still myself before you, Father, and wait patiently for you. I will not fret when others succeed in their ways and carry out wicked schemes.

Help me to be completely humble and patient, to be gentle and to forbear with others in love. As one of your chosen people, Father, I will clothe myself with compassion, kindness, humility, gentleness, and patience. Through your grace I will forgive whatever grievances I have toward others. I want to learn to forgive, Lord, as you have forgiven me.

Help me to warn those who are idle, encourage the timid, help the weak, and be patient with all people. With your help I will pursue patience, righteousness, godliness, faith, love, endurance, and gentleness. Thank you, Father.

Through the power of your Holy Spirit I will add goodness to my faith, knowledge to my goodness, self-control to my knowledge, patience and perseverance to my self-control, and godliness to my patience and perseverance.

Help me to remember to rejoice in the midst of hardships and suffering, realizing that suffering produces patience and perseverance, perseverance produces character, and character produces hope.

Father, as I wait and hope for what I do not have, I do so patiently, because I know you will supply all my need according to your riches in glory by Christ Jesus. Help me to be joyful in hope, patient in affliction, and faithful in prayer.

It is my desire, Father, to live a life that is worthy of you. I want to please you in every way, bear fruit in every good work, grow in the knowledge of you, and be strengthened with all power according to your glorious might so that I will have great endurance and patience with joy.

Help me never to be lazy, but to imitate those who through faith and patience have inherited what you've promised to them. Show me how to persevere so that when I have done your will, I will receive what you have promised to me.

Thank you, Father, for all the promises of your Word. Believing in them gives me great peace and patience.

Scriptures: 1 Corinthians 13:4; Psalm 37:7; Ephesians 4:2; Colossians 3:12; 1 Thessalonians 5:14; 2 Peter 1:5; Romans 5:3; Romans 8:25; Philippians 4:19; Romans 12:12; Colossians 1:10; Hebrews 10:36.

Personal Affirmation: I will be patient, for this is acceptable to the Lord. (See 1 Peter 2:20.)

Meditation: *"Have patience with all things, but chiefly have patience with yourself. Do not lose courage in considering your imperfections, but instantly set about remedying them—every day begin the task anew"* (St. Francis de Sales).

41

PEACE

Depart from evil, and do good; seek peace, and pursue it. (Psalm 34:14)

Central Focus: Peace with God, with others, and with ourselves brings happiness into our lives. God promises peace to us; it is our job to receive it and walk in it.

A Promise From God: "My son, forget not my law; but let thine heart keep my commandments. For length of days, and long life, and peace, shall they add to thee" (Proverbs 3:1-2).

Prayer: Lord, you are the Prince of peace. Thank you for the good news of peace that comes to us through our Lord Jesus Christ, who is the Lord of all. Thank you for justifying me through faith and giving me peace with you through Him.

Thank you for imparting strength to me and blessing me with peace. Your promises give me peace. I thank you for your promise that tells me that you provide health and healing for me, and you will let me enjoy abundant peace and security.

Great God of hope, fill me with all joy and peace as I learn to trust you, so that I will overflow with hope in the power of the Holy Spirit.

Instead of being anxious, I will give thanks in everything and I will let my requests be made known unto you.

As I do so, your wonderful peace that surpasses all understanding will guard my heart and my mind through Christ Jesus. Thank you, Father.

Lord of peace, thank you so much for your promise to give me peace at all times and in every way. I receive it now as I pray. The peace that Jesus gives to me is so terrific. He does not give as the world gives, so I will not let my heart be troubled or afraid.

Thank you for overcoming the world, Lord. Though there is trouble in the world, in you I have great peace. You are my peace. Thank you for destroying the barrier, the dividing wall of hostility, by abolishing in your flesh the Law with its commandments and regulations.

I will let your peace rule in my heart. Thank you for calling me to peace. I shall ever be thankful for all you've provided for me. Thank you for letting me into your kingdom, a kingdom that does not consist of eating and drinking, but of righteousness, peace, and joy in the Holy Spirit. Thank you, Father.

In the name of the Prince of Peace I pray, Amen.

Scriptures: Isaiah 9:6; Acts 10:36; Romans 5:1; Psalm 29:11; Jeremiah 33:6; Romans 15:13; Philippians 4:7; John 14:27; John 16:33; Ephesians 2:14–15; Romans 14:17.

Personal Affirmation: Through Jesus Christ I accept God's peace, which passes all understanding.

Meditation: *"Rest is not a hallowed feeling that comes over us in church; it is the repose of a heart set deep in God"* (Henry Drummond).

42
POWER

*He giveth power to the faint; and to them that
have no might he increaseth strength. . . .But they
that wait upon the Lord shall renew their strength;
they shall mount up with wings as eagles; they
shall run, and not be weary; and they shall walk
and not faint.* (Isaiah 40:29-31)

Central Focus: God's power is greater than anything
else. Through His power we are able to overcome and
prevail. His power and His might are at work in our
lives as we pray.

A Promise From God: "Now unto him that is able to
do exceeding abundantly above all that we ask or
think, according to the power that worketh in us"
(Ephesians 3:20).

Prayer: Thank you, Father, for your all-sufficient grace
and for the fact that your power is made perfect in my
weakness. Let your power rest upon me. How I praise
you for your incomparably great power that is at
work in my life. Your power comes from your mighty
strength, which you exerted in Christ when you raised
Him from the dead and seated Him at your right hand
in the heavens.

Thank you for your power that comes through the Holy
Spirit and enables me to be an effective witness for
you. You give strength to the weary and you increase

the power of the weak. I hope in you, Lord, and I know you are renewing my strength. Thank you for enabling me to soar like an eagle. Through your power I will run and not be weary and I shall walk and not faint. Thank you, Father.

How I praise you that you have not given me a spirit of timidity, but one of power, love, and self-control. Hallelujah! Thank you for the gift of your grace which has been given to me by the effectual working of your power.

My desire is to know Christ and the power of His resurrection. I want to join the fellowship of His sufferings and be made conformable unto His death. I have received Jesus Christ as my Lord and Savior, and He has given me the power to become a child of God, because I believe on His name. Thank you, Father.

Your right hand, O Lord, has become glorious in power, and it has dashed the enemy in pieces. Thank you, Lord. I will sing unto you, because you have triumphed gloriously. The horse and his rider you have thrown into the sea.

You are my strength and my song, and you have become my salvation. You are my God, and I will prepare a habitation for you. You are my father's God, and I exalt you. You are a man of war. You are my refuge and my strength, a very present help in trouble. Therefore, I will not fear.

Lord, you reign and you are clothed with majesty and strength. I wait upon you, O Lord, and, as I do so, you impart your courage to me and you strengthen my heart. Thank you for your power which is at work in my life.

Now unto you who are able to do exceeding abundantly above all that I ask or think, according to your power that is at work within me, unto you be glory by Christ Jesus throughout all ages, world without end.

In the powerful name of Jesus I pray, Amen.

Scriptures: 2 Corinthians 12:9; Ephesians 1:9; Acts 1:8; Isaiah 40:29-31; 2 Timothy 1:7; Ephesians 3:7; Philippians 3:10; Exodus 15:6; Exodus 15:2-3; Psalm 46:1-2; Psalm 93:1; Psalm 27:14; Ephesians 3:20-21.

Personal Affirmation: It is God's power, not my own, that has enabled me to overcome and prevail. He has given me power to run the good race to the end. My strength is renewed by His power.

Meditation: *"The power of God is available to you today to help you do whatever you need to do and with a smile on your face"* (Joyce Meyer).

43

PRAISE

O Lord, open thou my lips; and my mouth shall shew forth thy praise. (Psalm 51:15)

Central Focus: God inhabits the praises of His people. Praise takes us from the problem to the power and peace of God. Praise brings forth a multitude of blessings in our lives.

A Promise From God: "Enter into his gates with thanksgiving, and into his courts with praise: be thankful unto him, and bless his name. For the Lord is good; his mercy is everlasting; and his truth endureth to all generations" (Psalm 100:4-5).

Prayer: O Lord God, thank you for the power of praise. You are so praiseworthy and I want to thank you in everything, for I know this is your will in Christ Jesus concerning me.

I will give thanks to you because of your righteousness, and I will sing praise to you, O Most High. Praise be to you, O Lord, for you are my strength and my shield. My heart fully trusts in you, and I am being helped. My heart leaps for joy and I will give thanks to you in song.

I will extoll you at all times, dear Lord, and your praise will always be upon my lips. My soul will boast in you and I will always exalt your name. Praise be to you, O Lord, the God of Israel, from everlasting to everlasting.

Praise awaits you, O Lord, in Zion. I will fulfill my vows to you. I give thanks to you, O God, for your name is near. I will tell of your wonderful deeds. I will sing for joy to you, for you are my strength. I will shout aloud to you.

I will sing to you all my life. I will sing praise to you as long as I live. May my meditation be pleasing to you, as I rejoice in you. I will exalt you, my God the King. I will praise your name forever and ever. Every day I will praise you and extoll your name.

Great are you, O Lord, and you are most worthy of praise. Your greatness is unfathomable. I will proclaim your good deeds. You are so gracious and compassionate. You are slow to anger and rich in love. You are good to all. Your kingdom is an everlasting kingdom, and your dominion endures throughout all generations. You are faithful to all your promises, and you are loving toward all that you have made.

You uphold all who fall, and you lift up all who are bowed down. You open your hands and satisfy the desires of every living thing. Thank you, Father. My mouth will speak in praise of you forever.

O Lord, you are my God. I will exalt you and praise your name, for in perfect faithfulness you have done marvelous things for me. Thank you for everything.

In Jesus' name I pray, Amen.

Scriptures: 1 Thessalonians 5:18; Psalm 7:17; Psalm 28:6; Psalm 34:1; Psalm 75:1; Psalm 81:1; Psalm 104:33; Psalm 145:1–21; Isaiah 25:1.

Personal Affirmation: I praise God all day long in everything.

Meditation: *"The happiness of the creature consists in rejoicing in God, by which also God is magnified and glorified"* (Jonathan Edwards).

44

RIGHTEOUSNESS

The righteous shall inherit the land, and dwell therein forever. The mouth of the righteous speaketh wisdom, and his tongue talketh of judgment. (Psalm 37:29-30)

Central Focus: As humans, we have no righteousness. As believers, we have the righteousness of Christ which has been imparted to us.

A Promise From God: "Being filled with the fruits of righteousness, which are by Jesus Christ, unto the glory and praise of God" (Philippians 1:11).

Prayer: O God, my heavenly Father, thank you for freeing me from sin and helping me to become a servant of righteousness. I ask that you would help me to put off the old man, which is corrupted through deceitful lusts and help me to be renewed in the spirit of my mind, as I put on the new man, which is created in righteousness and true holiness.

Thank you for your promise which tells me that those who hunger and thirst after righteousness shall be filled. I hunger and thirst after your righteousness, Father, and I thank you for making it a possible attainment for me.

Help me to walk worthy of you unto all pleasing, being fruitful in every good work, and increasing in the knowledge of you. Strengthen me with all might, according to your glorious power, unto all patience and longsuffering with joyfulness. I give thanks unto you, Father, for making me meet to be a partaker of the inheritance of the saints in light. Thank you for delivering me from the power of darkness and translating me into the kingdom of your dear Son.

It comforts me to know that your eyes are upon me and your ears are attentive to my cry. I hate evil, Father, and I thank you so much that you guard my life and deliver me from the hand of the wicked. Thank you so much for shedding your light upon me and giving me deep and abiding joy.

I pray that my love will abound more and more in knowledge and all judgment. Fill me with the fruits of righteousness, which are by Jesus Christ unto your glory and praise. With your help I will make every effort to add goodness to my faith, knowledge to my goodness, self-control to my knowledge, perseverance to my self-control, godliness to my perseverance, brotherly kindness to my godliness, and love to my brotherly kindness.

Thank you for sending Jesus, Father, for He is made unto me wisdom, righteousness, sanctification, and redemption. Praise your name, Lord. You are my Shepherd; I shall not want. You make me to lie down in green pastures, and you lead me beside the still waters. You restore my soul, and lead me in the paths of righteousness for your name's sake. Thank you, Lord.

Surely goodness and mercy shall follow me all the days of my life, and I will dwell in your house forever.

In Jesus' righteous name I pray, Amen.

Scriptures: Romans 6:18; Ephesians 4:23; Matthew 5:6; Colossians 1:10–13; Psalm 34:15; Psalm 97:10; Philippians 1:10–11; 2 Peter 1:5–8; 1 Corinthians 1:30; Psalm 23.

Personal Affirmation: The Bible says, "There is none righteous, no, not one" (Romans 3:10). So I have no righteousness of my own. As a believer, however, the righteousness of Christ has been imparted to me and I am filled by its fruits.

Meditation: *"Rest assured: Before God, the righteousness of Christ is all we need; before God, the righteousness of Christ is all we have"* (Tullian Tchividjian).

45

SPEECH

*But the tongue can no man tame; it is an unruly
evil, full of deadly poison. Therewith bless we
God, even the Father; and therewith curse we
men, which are made after the similitude of God.*
(James 3:8-9)

Central Focus: The control of our tongues is one of
life's biggest challenges. Our tongues truly do possess
the power of life and death for our lives as well as
those of others. (See Proverbs 18:21.) God will help us
control our tongues.

A Promise From God: "Let your speech be always with
grace, seasoned with salt, that ye may know how ye
ought to answer every man" (Colossians 4:6).

Prayer: Father, I thank you for the gift of speech. Help
me to use it to glorify you and bless others. May I never
let any unwholesome speech come from my mouth,
but only that which is helpful for edifying others and
encouraging them.

Instead of engaging in slander, gossip, foolish talk,
obscenity, or coarse joking, I want to use the gift
of speech to offer thanksgiving to you. May I never
slander anyone. I want to be peaceable, considerate,
and humble in my relationships with others.

Through your grace I will never repay evil with evil

or insult with insult, but with blessing, because you have called me to blessing, that I would inherit your blessing. Thank you for your blessings in my life, Lord. Father, I hate pride, arrogance, evil behavior, and perverse speech.

Help me to keep my tongue from evil and my lips from speaking lies. Show me how to put perversity away from my mouth, and to keep corrupt speech far from my lips. May I simply let my yes be yes and my no be no, for I realize that anything else comes from the evil one.

May my mouth be a fountain of life. Help me to remember that sin is usually found in the multitude of words; help me to control my speech. May my mouth bring forth wisdom at all times. Let me be a truthful witness, Father. Keep me from ever speaking reckless words, which pierce like a sword. May my tongue always bring healing.

Help me to guard my lips and thereby guard my life. May I never speak rashly. May I always remember that a gentle answer turns wrath away, but a harsh word stirs up anger. Help me to use my tongue to spread knowledge.

I know, Father, that I find joy when I give an apt reply. How good is a timely word. Thank you for showing me that pleasant words are a honeycomb, sweet to the soul and healing to the bones. Hallelujah!

It is my desire to be a person of knowledge who uses

words with restraint. I believe your Word which tells me that when I guard my mouth and my tongue I will be able to avoid calamity. May my speech always be gracious.

I want my words to always be aptly spoken, like apples of gold in settings of silver. May my words ever be wise, wholesome, full of grace, just, truthful, gentle, timely, pleasant, and quiet. In this way I will be a good witness to others and I will glorify you, Father.

In the wonderful name of Jesus I pray, Amen.

Scriptures: Ephesians 4:29; Ephesians 5:4; Titus 3:2; 1 Peter 3:9; Proverbs 8:13; Psalm 34:13; Proverbs 4:24; Proverbs 10:11; Proverbs 10:19; Proverbs 10:31; Proverbs 12:17-18; Proverbs 13:3; Proverbs 15:1; Proverbs 15:7; Proverbs 15:23; Proverbs 16:24; Proverbs 17:27; Proverbs 21:23; Proverbs 22:11; Proverbs 25:11; Proverbs 15:2; Ephesians 4:29; Colossians 4:6; Psalm 37:30; Proverbs 12:19; Proverbs 15:1; Proverbs 15:23; Proverbs 16:24; Ecclesiastes 9:17.

Personal Affirmation: I will use my speech to praise God and to edify and uplift others. I will speak the truth in love and avoid slander, lies, and negative speech. With my speech I will bless God and others and give thanks.

Meditation: *"Kind words produce their images on men's souls"* (Blaise Pascal).

46

TEMPTATION

There hath no temptation taken you but such as is common to man: But God is faithful, who will not suffer you to be tempted above that ye are able; but will with the temptation also make a way to escape, that ye may be able to bear it. (1 Corinthians 10:13)

Central Focus: When temptations come our way we can either resist them or yield to them. The Bible says, "Submit yourselves therefore to God. Resist the devil, and he will flee from you. Draw nigh to God, and he will draw near to you" (James 4:7–8). When we follow the steps outlined by James we will be able to rise above every temptation.

A Promise From God: "Blessed is the man that endureth temptation: for when he is tried, he shall receive the crown of life, which the Lord hath promised to them that love him" (James 1:12).

Prayer: Heavenly Father, I thank you for the power you've given to me to resist all temptation. Help me to apply your power to my life whenever temptation comes my way. Instead of being overcome by evil, I will overcome evil with good.

I submit my life to you, Father, and I resist the devil, knowing that he will flee from me. As I draw near to you, I know you are drawing near to me. Thank you,

Lord. Help me to be self-controlled and alert at all times, because my enemy, the devil, prowls around like a roaring lion, and he is looking for someone to devour. Standing firm in the faith, I will resist him, and I know you will always enable me overcome him.

Thank you, Lord, for always giving me your help. Your love supports me. Thank you for the wisdom you are imparting to me. The knowledge you give to me is pleasant to my soul. I know that discretion will protect me and understanding will guard me. Your wisdom will save me from the ways of wicked men, and from all whose ways and words are perverse.

Help me always to remember that the lust of the flesh, the lust of the eyes, and the pride of life comes from the world and not from you. May I never set my feet on the path of the wicked or walk in the way of evil persons.

Thank you for your promise to those who persevere under trial. I know, Father, that when I stand the test, I will receive the crown of life you have promised to all who love you. I greatly rejoice in you, for even when I have to suffer grief for a while, my faith is greatly strengthened, and the testing is of greater worth than gold, which perishes even when it is refined by fire.

May my faith ever be proved genuine and may it result in praise, glory, and honor when Jesus Christ is revealed.

Thank you for faith, Father, which is the victory that overcomes the world. I will walk in faith every step of my way.

Through the powerful name of Jesus I pray, Amen.

Scriptures: Romans 12:1; James 4:7–8; 1 Peter 5:8–9; Psalm 94:17; Proverbs 2:10–12; 1 John 2:16; Proverbs 4:14; James 1:12; 1 Peter 1:6–7; 1 John 5:4.

Personal Affirmation: I am tempted every day. But I know that every temptation is common to others and that God has provided a way to escape temptation. I choose to submit to God, resist temptation, and focus on other, more positive, ways to endure it.

Meditation: *"Faith is to believe what you do not see; the reward of this faith is to see what you believe"* (Augustine).

47

THANKFULNESS

Rejoice evermore. Pray without ceasing.
In everything give thanks: for this is the will of God
in Christ Jesus concerning you.
(1 Thessalonians 5:16–18)

Central Focus: The abundant blessings of God are always there for you. Focus on them, not on any problems your may be experiencing, and your burden will grow smaller. Praise and thanksgiving lift you out of the darkness of despair.

A Promise From God: "For all things are for your sakes, that the abundant grace might through the thanksgiving of many redound to the glory of God" (2 Corinthians 4:15).

Prayer: I give thanks to you, O Lord, for you are good. Your love endures forever. I thank you for your unfailing love and for all your wonderful deeds. I will praise you, O Lord, with all my heart. I will tell of all your wonders. I will be glad and rejoice in you, my dear Father. I will sing praise to your name, O Most High!

You are my strength and my shield. My heart trusts in you, and I am helped. My heart leaps for joy, and I will give you thanks in song. I will extoll you, O Lord, for you have lifted me up, and you have not allowed my enemies to triumph over me. Hallelujah! I cried unto you, and you helped me. Thank you, Father.

You have brought up my soul from the grave and kept me alive. I will sing unto you, and I will give thanks at the remembrance of your holiness. Praise your matchless name! Thank you for turning my mourning into dancing and girding me with gladness to the end that my glory may sing praise to you and not be silent. O Lord my God, I will give thanks to you forever.

Lord, I've waited patiently for you. Thank you for inclining your ear to me and hearing my cry. Thank your for bringing me up also out of a horrible pit, out of the miry clay, and setting my feet upon a rock and establishing my goings.

Thank you for putting a new song in my mouth, even praise unto you, my God. Many shall see it and trust in you. Great are you, O Lord, and greatly to be praised. It is a good thing to give thanks to you, Father, and to sing praises unto your name, O Most High. I love you, Father. You have made me glad through your work, and I will triumph in the work of your hands.

I come before your presence with thanksgiving, and I make a joyful noise to you with Psalms, for you are a great God and a great King above all gods. In your hand are the deep places of the Earth, and the strength of the hills is yours also. The sea is yours, and you made it. Your hands formed the dry land.

I worship and bow down before you, Father. I kneel before you, for you are my Maker. You are my God, and I am a sheep in your pasture. I will make a joyful noise unto you, O God, and I will serve you with gladness, as I come before your presence with singing.

I know you are my God. You made me and fashioned me after your image. I enter into your gates with thanksgiving and into your courts with praise. I am thankful unto you, as I bless your holy name. You are so good, and your truth endures to all generations.

In the blessed name of Jesus I pray, Amen.

Scriptures: Psalm 107:1; Psalm 107:15; Psalm 9:1-2; Psalm 28:7; Psalm 30; Psalm 40:1-3; Psalm 48:1; Psalm 92:1; Psalm 95:1-7; Psalm 100.

Personal Affirmation: I am so thankful for everything the Lord has given me and done for me. Even when I am feeling low, I focus on the many blessings in my life, the trials the Lord has brought me through, and the triumphs He has provided. Thankfulness soon lifts my spirits and I praise God.

Meditation: *"Perhaps it takes a purer faith to praise God for unrealized blessings than for those we once enjoyed or those we enjoy now"* (A.W. Tozer).

———— ◆◆◆◆ ————

48

WISDOM

*Happy is the man that findeth wisdom, and the
man that getteth understanding.* (Proverbs 3:13)

Central Focus: All wisdom comes from God. Therefore,
to get wisdom we must get to know Him. His wisdom
is vital and it is worth more than silver, gold, rubies,
or any precious commodity. God gives wisdom when
we seek Him and His ways.

A Promise From God: "When wisdom entereth into
thine heart, and knowledge is pleasant unto thy soul;
discretion shall preserve thee, understanding shall keep
thee" (Proverbs 2:10–11).

Prayer: O God, my heavenly Father and source of all
wisdom, I come to you now to ask for wisdom in all the
decisions and choices of my life. Thank you for your
promise to give wisdom to me, as I come to you in faith.

May my lips spread both wisdom and knowledge.
Father, as I get wisdom from you, I am giving regard
and love to my own soul. I cherish understanding,
and this brings prosperity to me. Thank you, Father.
Help me to listen to advice and to accept instruction,
for I know this will bring wisdom to me.

May I never forget that wisdom is better than the
weapons of war, gold, silver, rubies, and strength. The
wisdom you've imparted to me, Father, blesses me

and makes me happy. Nothing I desire can compare with wisdom.

Long life, riches, honor, and peace are supplied to me through wisdom. Its ways are pleasant and its paths lead to peace. Wisdom is a tree of life to me. Thank you for your secret wisdom, a wisdom that has been hidden and that you destined for me before time began.

Let me show your wisdom by a good life and by deeds done in humility. Through your grace I will let the word of Christ dwell in me richly. Help me to teach and admonish others with all wisdom.

Thank you for your wisdom which is pure, peace-loving, considerate, submissive, full of mercy and good fruit, impartial, and sincere. I will walk in your wisdom, Father. Teach me your ways, O Lord, and I will walk in your wisdom and truth. Give me an undivided heart, that I may fear, honor, and respect you.

I praise you for the full riches of understanding that you have given to me. This will enable me to know your mystery, Father, and to know Christ more fully. In Him are hidden all the treasures of wisdom and knowledge. Thank you, God.

Fill me with the knowledge of your will through all spiritual wisdom and understanding. May I ever live a life that is worthy of you. I want to please you in every way and bear fruit in every good work, as I grow in my knowledge of you.

May I never forget that a house is built by wisdom and

it is established by understanding. Through knowledge its rooms are filled with rare and beautiful treasures. Thank you for the power and strength your wisdom gives to me.

Eye has not seen and ear has not heard, neither have entered into the human heart, the things you've prepared for all those who love you. Thank you for revealing these things to me by your Spirit, and I thank you that your Spirit searches all things, including the deep, spiritual things. Help me never to speak in man's wisdom, Father, but only in the wisdom of the Holy Spirit.

In the wise name of Jesus I pray, Amen.

Scriptures: James 1:3–6; Proverbs 15:7; Proverbs 19:8; Proverbs 19:20; Ecclesiastes 9:13–18; 1 Corinthians 2:7–8; James 3:13; Colossians 3:16; James 3:17; Psalm 86:11; Colossians 2:1; Colossians 1:9–10; Proverbs 24:3–5; 1 Corinthians 2:9–14.

Personal Affirmation: I come to the Lord every day for wisdom and I seek understanding. I gain knowledge by spending time with God in prayer and by reading His Word in the Bible.

Meditation: *"Never mistake knowledge for wisdom. One helps you make a living; the other helps you make a life"* (Sandra Carey).

49

WORD OF GOD

Thy word is a lamp unto my feet, and a light unto my path. (Psalm 119:105)

Central Focus: God's Word has been aptly called the Manufacturer's Handbook, and I will walk in the light this book shines in front of me. God's Word is truth, and is the sword of the Spirit. God's Word and its promises impart life, wisdom, happiness, and wholeness to me.

A Promise From God: "Thy word have I hid in my heart, that I might not sin against thee" (Psalm 119:11).

Prayer: Dear Father, I thank you for your glorious Word. It makes me wise unto salvation through faith in Jesus Christ. Hallelujah! My delight is in your Word, and I will meditate upon it each step of my way. Help me to ever do what your Word says.

Your Word is living and active. It is sharper than any two-edged sword and is able to penetrate ever to the dividing of the soul from the spirit. It judges my thoughts and intents. Thank you, Father, for your Word.

I will let your Word dwell in me richly, as I teach and admonish others with the wisdom your Word imparts. Help me to do my best to show myself a workman who never needs to be ashamed, because I know how to rightly divide your Word.

Your Word, O Father, is like fire and like a hammer

that breaks the rock in pieces. I want to be like the Bereans who studied the Scriptures daily. I will listen to your words, Lord, and abide by them. Strengthen me according to your Word.

I have placed all my hope in your Word. How sweet are your words to my taste, sweeter than honey to my mouth. Through your Word I gain understanding. Direct my footsteps according to your Word. Let no sin rule over me. All your promises have been thoroughly tested, and I love them so much.

All Scripture has been given by you, Father, and all Scripture is profitable for teaching, rebuking, correcting, and training in righteousness, so that I may be thoroughly equipped for every good work. Thank you for cleansing me through your Word. Thank you for renewing my mind through your Word.

In Jesus' name I pray, Amen.

Scriptures: 2 Timothy 3:15; Psalm 1:2; James 1:22; Hebrews 4:12; Colossians 3:16; 2 Timothy 2:15; Jeremiah 23:29; Acts 17:11; Psalm 78:1; Psalm 119:28; Psalm 119:74; Psalm 119:103; Psalm 119:133; Psalm 119:140; 2 Timothy 3:16; John 15:3.

Personal Affirmation: I delight in God's Word. It lights my way and leads me in the direction God wants me to go.

Meditation: *"The soul can do without everything except the Word of God, without which none at all of its wants are provided for"* (Martin Luther).

50
WORSHIP

O come, let us worship and bow down: let us kneel before the Lord our maker. (Psalm 95:6)

Central Focus: Through worship we get to know God as He is. We worship Him for who He is, and we praise him for all He has done. He is worthy of all our worship.

A Promise From God: "Exalt ye the Lord our God, and worship at his footstool; for he is holy" (Psalm 99:5).

Prayer: Father God, I worship you. I ascribe glory to your name, as I come before you and worship you in the splendor of holiness. I exalt you as I worship at your footstool, for I know you are holy. I shout for joy to you, and I worship you with gladness, as I come before you with joyful songs.

Help me to worship you in spirit and truth, for I know this is what you want. You are my strength and my song. You have become my salvation. You are my God, and I will praise and worship you. I will exalt your name forever.

One thing I ask of you, Lord God, and this is what I seek: that I may dwell in your house all the days of my life, gazing upon your beauty, and worshipping you in your holy temple. Better is one day in your house, O Lord, than a thousand elsewhere. I would rather be a doorkeeper in your house than dwell in the tents of the wicked.

How lovely is your dwelling place, O Lord, the Almighty! My soul yearns, even faints, for your courts. My heart and my soul cry out for you. I lift up holy hands unto you. I shout for joy unto you, O Lord, and I worship you with gladness. I come before your presence in worship. You are my God. You are my Creator. I am a sheep in your pasture.

I enter into your gates with thanksgiving and go into your courts with praise. I am thankful unto you, and I bless your holy name. You are good, and your mercy is everlasting. Your truth endures to all generations.

Bless you, Lord. You are so great. You are clothed with honor and majesty. I give thanks to you, as I call upon your name and make your deeds known to others. I sing unto you and I talk of all your wondrous works. I glory in your holy name and I rejoice as I seek you.

As I worship you, I remember all your marvelous works, your wonders, and the judgments of your mouth. I love you, Father, because you have heard my voice and my supplications. Thank you for inclining your ear unto me. I will call upon you as long as I live.

O Lord, truly I am your servant. I am the son of your handmaiden. Thank you for loosing my bonds. I will offer to you the sacrifice of thanksgiving, and I will call upon your name. I will pay my vows unto you and worship you in the presence of your people.

My worship belongs to you alone, O Lord.

Scriptures: 1 Chronicles 16:29; Psalm 99:5; Psalm 100:1;

John 4:23–24; Exodus 15:2; Psalm 27:4; Psalm 84:1–2; 1 Timothy 2:8; Psalm 100:1; Psalm 100:2–5; Psalm 104:1; Psalm 105:1–5; Psalm 116:1–2; Psalm 116:16–19.

Personal Affirmation: I kneel before the Lord and worship Him, for He is worthy of my adoration.

Meditation: *"A man can no more diminish God's glory by refusing to worship Him than a lunatic can put out the sun by scribbling the word 'darkness' on the walls of his cell"* (C.S. Lewis).

More "Prayers That Change Things"
by Lloyd Hildebrand

More than 100,000 copies of the books in this series have been sold! These mass-market paperbacks contain prayers that are built from the promises of God and teaching that is thoroughly scriptural.

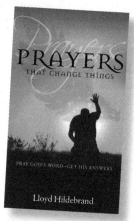

ISBN: 978-1-61036-105-7
MMP / 192 pages

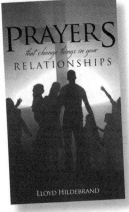

ISBN: 978-0-88270-012-0
MMP / 232 pages

ISBN: 978-0-88270-743-3
MMP / 232 pages

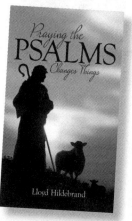

ISBN: 978-1-61036-126-2
MMP / 216 pages